The
Space Race

Titles in the World History Series

WORLD
HISTORY SERIES

The
Space Race

by
Nathan Aaseng

Lucent Books, P.O. Box 289011, San Diego, CA 92198-9011

Library of Congress Cataloging-in-Publication Data

Aaseng, Nathan.
    The Space Race / by Nathan Aaseng.
        p. cm.—(World history series)
    Summary: Explores the history of rocketry, including the
race between the United States and the Soviet Union to land
men on the moon.
    ISBN 1-56006-809-4 (hardback : alk. paper)
    1. Space race—Juvenile literature. 2. Astronautics—United
States—Juvenile literature. 3. Astronautics—Soviet Union—
Juvenile literature. [1. Space race. 2. Astronautics—United
States—History. 3. Astrounautics—Soviet Union—History.] I.
Title. II. Series.
    TL793 .A233 2002
    629.4'0973—dc21

00-013235

Contents

Foreword

Each year on the first day of school, nearly every history teacher faces the task of explaining why his or her students should study history. One logical answer to this question is that exploring what happened in our past explains how the things we often take for granted—our customs, ideas, and institutions—came to be. As statesman and historian Winston Churchill put it, "Every nation or group of nations has its own tale to tell. Knowledge of the trials and struggles is necessary to all who would comprehend the problems, perils, challenges, and opportunities which confront us today." Thus, a study of history puts modern ideas and institutions in perspective. For example, though the founders of the United States were talented and creative thinkers, they clearly did not invent the concept of democracy. Instead, they adapted some democratic ideas that had originated in ancient Greece and with which the Romans, the British, and others had experimented. An exploration of these cultures, then, reveals their very real connection to us through institutions that continue to shape our daily lives.

Another reason often given for studying history is the idea that lessons exist in the past from which contemporary societies can benefit and learn. This idea, although controversial, has always been an intriguing one for historians. Those who agree that society can benefit from the past often quote philosopher George Santayana's famous statement, "Those who cannot remember the past are condemned to repeat it." Historians who subscribe to Santayana's philosophy believe that, for example, studying the events that led up to the major world wars or other significant historical events would allow society to chart a different and more favorable course in the future.

Just as difficult as convincing students to realize the importance of studying history is the search for useful and interesting supplementary materials that present historical events in a context that can be easily understood. The volumes in Lucent Books' World History Series attempt to present a broad, balanced, and penetrating view of the march of history. Ancient Egypt's important wars and rulers, for example, are presented against the rich and colorful backdrop of Egyptian religious, social, and cultural developments. The series engages the reader by enhancing historical events with these cultural contexts. For example, in *Ancient Greece*, the text covers the role of women in that society. Slavery is discussed in *The Roman Empire*, as well as how slaves earned their freedom. The numerous and varied aspects of everyday life in these and other societies are explored in each volume of the series. Additionally, the series covers the major political, cultural, and philosophical ideas as the torch of civilization is passed from ancient Mesopotamia and Egypt, through Greece, Rome, Medieval Europe, and other world cultures, to the modern day.

The material in the series is formatted in a thorough, precise, and organized manner. Each volume offers the reader a comprehensive and clearly written overview of an important historical event or period. The topic under discussion is placed in a broad, historical context. For example, The Italian Renaissance begins with a discussion of the High Middle Ages and the loss of central control that allowed certain Italian cities to develop artistically. The book ends by looking forward to the Reformation and interpreting the societal changes that grew out of the Renaissance. Thus, students are not only involved in an historical era, but also enveloped by the events leading up to that era and the events following it.

One important and unique feature in the World History Series is the primary and secondary source quotations that richly supplement each volume. These quotes are useful in a number of ways. First, they allow students access to sources they would not normally be exposed to because of the difficulty and obscurity of the original source. The quotations range from interesting anecdotes to farsighted cultural perspectives and are drawn from historical witnesses both past and present. Second, the quotes demonstrate how and where historians themselves derive their information on the past as they strive to reach a consensus on historical events. Lastly, all of the quotes are footnoted, familiarizing students with the citation process and allowing them to verify quotes and/or look up the original source if the quote piques their interest.

Finally, the books in the World History Series provide a detailed launching point for further research. Each book contains a bibliography specifically geared toward student research. A second, annotated bibliography introduces students to all the sources the author consulted when compiling the book. A chronology of important dates gives students an overview, at a glance, of the topic covered. Where applicable, a glossary of terms is included.

In short, the series is designed not only to acquaint readers with the basics of history, but also to make them aware that their lives are a part of an ongoing human saga. Perhaps they will then come to the same realization as famed historian Arnold Toynbee. In his monumental work, *A Study of History*, he wrote about becoming aware of history flowing through him in a mighty current, and of his own life "welling like a wave in the flow of this vast tide."

Sparks of the Space Race

In the beginning space travel was a flight of wishful imagination. Untold centuries ago, some unknown person looked up at the moon, a glowing disk in the night sky, and wondered what it would be like to travel to such a place. About 1,850 years ago, a Greek named Lucian wrote down the first fictional account of travel to another world. During the centuries that followed, a journey to the moon and other planets remained a popular fantasy theme of writers.

Little did these writers know that work on the engine that would eventually carry humans to the moon had been going on since even before the time of Lucian. As early as the second century B.C., the Chinese discovered that igniting black powder—a mixture of charcoal, sulfur, and saltpeter—could propel an object through the air with tremendous force. By the thirteenth century, the Chinese had achieved sufficient control over the direction of these devices, known as rockets, that they were commonly used both in celebration and as military weapons.

FROM WISHFUL THINKING TO PLAUSIBLE DREAM

Serious consideration of these small, explosive devices as a means of transporting people into space did not occur until another fiction writer, Frenchman Jules Verne, incorporated them into his work. In 1865 Verne wrote a book called *From the Earth to the Moon*, in which he described a lunar landing by three space travelers from earth. What made Verne's book different from previous fiction efforts was that he packed his account full of scientific details that made the voyage seem plausible. In the words of the twentieth-century rocket scientist Wernher von Braun, "He was read with great respect by working scientists, so carefully did he do his scientific homework."[1] Verne's work was followed by British writer H. G. Wells, who penned another realistic moon shot, *The First Men in the Moon*, at the turn of the twentieth century.

RUSSIAN PIONEER

The works of these authors sparked an unquenchable curiosity in thousands of young readers, many of whom were inspired to pursue scientific careers. Among them was a Russian scientist and schoolteacher named Konstantin Tsiolkovsky, born in 1857. Tsiolkovsky originally focused on designing airplanes, but in 1895 he shifted his interest to working on spaceships. He was the first to apply mathematics and physics to the notion of rocket flight into outer space.

Tsiolkovsky wrote,

> For a long time I thought of the rocket as everybody else did—just as a means of diversion and of petty everyday uses. I do not remember exactly what prompted me to make calcula-

This illustration from Jules Verne's From the Earth to the Moon *shows three space travelers standing on the moon.*

tion of its motions. Probably the first seeds of the idea were sown by that great fantastic author Jules Verne—he directed my thought along certain channels—then came a desire, and after that, the work of the mind."[2]

In 1898 Tsiolkovsky sent a paper detailing his work on theories and principles governing rocket propulsion to *Science Survey*. One of his most innovative proposals in that article was that the most efficient propellants for a rocket could be liquid oxygen and liquid hydrogen. In this, Tsiolkovsky was decades ahead of his time. British researcher James Dewar had only recently prepared the first samples of liquid hydrogen. Rocket experts would not be able to harness the power of these ultracold substances for practical use until 1960.

Science Survey was unimpressed with Tsiolkovsky's work. The Russian magazine waited five years before publishing the article, by which time Tsiolkovsky had calculated the speed a rocket would need to achieve to break free from the earth's gravity. Even when it was finally published, Tsiolkovsky's article attracted little attention, except among a small group of science writers.

AMERICAN PIONEER

While Tsiolkovsky's work languished in obscurity, an American physics professor was blazing his own lonely trail in rocket science. In 1899 seventeen-year-old Robert Goddard, an avid reader of science fiction, climbed a ladder to trim a cherry tree.

THE UNITED STATES' ROCKET MAN

Robert Goddard carried out most of his experiments in the wide open spaces of New Mexico. By 1930 he was able to fire a rocket to two thousand feet, traveling at more than five hundred miles per hour. In 1935 he launched a rocket that traveled faster than the speed of sound. During his life he accumulated over 210 patents having to do with nearly every phase of rocket development.

In the meantime, Germany sent prying eyes of its own to the United States to examine the work of Robert Goddard. In contrast to the U.S. military, which showed no interest in Goddard's work, the Germans were astounded by reports that this lone man had advanced further in rocket science than the entire German program. In 1936 a spy named Gustav Guellich traveled to New Mexico and secretly watched as Goddard launched a rocket into the sky. He collected as many details as he could from Goddard's work and brought the information back to Germany.

Among Goddard's insights was a gyroscopic guidance system that controlled the direction of the flight. When the rocket's gyroscope sensed that the rocket was veering away from a vertical direction, it caused heat-resistant fins to dip into the rocket exhaust, which straightened out the flight. Goddard also developed a system that sent a film of alcohol along the rocket engine's walls to keep the rocket from overheating. He was also working on the problem of constructing lightweight turbo pumps to keep fuel flowing into the rocket engine, although with limited success.

Exactly how much the Germans learned from Goddard and how much they developed on their own is in dispute. They certainly perfected techniques such as alcohol cooling for which Goddard had only scratched the surface. Von Braun and his team succeeded where Goddard had stumbled in devising a means of delivering a steady stream of propellant to the engine. Engineer Walter Thiel invented the key component, a turbo pump driven by hydrogen peroxide, that efficiently delivered fuel from giant storage tanks to the combustion chamber. Nonetheless, when the United States captured one of von Braun's rockets later in the war, they were astounded at how closely it resembled Goddard's versions.

Robert Goddard poses next to one of his early rockets. In 1920 he launched the first rocket that used liquid fuel instead of powder.

require air and that, therefore, a rocket engine could function in outer space. Four years later, while working as a physics professor at Clark University in Massachusetts, he sent a proposal entitled "A Method of Reaching Extreme Altitudes" to the Smithsonian Institute. The institute was so impressed that it awarded him a $5,000 grant to put his theories and calculations into practice.

When the Smithsonian published Goddard's proposal in 1920, however, it proved a public relations disaster. The press focused on Goddard's brief mention of rocket flight to the moon and labeled him a crackpot. Stunned by the media attention and public scorn, Goddard kept a veil of secrecy over his work ever after. Working largely on his own, he built a ten-pound rocket with an engine fueled by two tanks—one filled with gasoline, the other with liquid oxygen. On March 16, with only his wife and two other observers present, he succeeded in launching the world's first liquid-fueled rocket on a 2.5-second burst that carried it forty-one feet into the air.

While looking down at the fields below, he suddenly was overwhelmed by a vision of traveling in space. Although the incident seems trivial, Goddard marked the date down on his calendar and wrote, "I was a different boy when I descended the ladder."[3] From that point on, he became obsessed with the idea of building rockets.

In 1912 Goddard proved mathematically that rocket fuel combustion did not

IRONY OF THE SPACE RACE

One of the supreme ironies of modern history is that the quest to conquer outer space began with these two men, one Russian and one American, toiling in isolation. Neither could get his government to take his work seriously. Not until the middle of the twentieth century did their respective nations, at almost the same moment, recognize the value of what Tsiolkovsky and

Goddard were doing. With the explosiveness of a rocket launch, both nations rose from indifference to a passionate desire to achieve superiority in space.

The space race between the United States and the Soviet Union that belatedly ignited from the sparks of their two lonely pioneers proved to be one of the most fascinating struggles of modern times. Unlike most heated international conflicts, it was resolved not by generals and their troops on the battlefield, but by scientists and engineers tapping the limits of human resourcefulness.

1 Military Interest in Rockets

In 1923 German professor Hermann Oberth independently reached the same conclusion as Tsiolkovsky and Goddard that modern liquid fuels offered far greater potential for rocket power than powder. The twenty-nine-year-old Oberth published at his own expense a short book in which he calculated the performance potential of propellants, such as gasoline and liquid oxygen, and offered suggestions for optimum design of a rocket ship. He concluded that many of the dreams of science fiction writers, such as manned spaceflight and orbiting space stations, were theoretically possible.

It was Oberth's book that ultimately triggered the space race between the United States and the Soviet Union, not because his ideas were so different from those of Tsiolkovsky and Goddard, but because, for the first time, those ideas attracted government interest. For although the dreamers and visionaries opened the door to the possibility of space travel, it was the power, resources, and will of powerful nations that made possible the tremendous and costly advances in science and technology that would place a man on the moon.

Following the publication of Oberth's book, the ageless dream of space travel evolved into a fierce struggle for world domination. Until the day that a human set foot on the moon, that race would be shaped and guided not by the thrill of adventure or the quest for scientific knowledge, but by international politics and national prestige.

WAKE-UP CALL

Hermann Oberth's book belatedly woke up the Soviet Union, into which Russia had been incorporated in 1917, to the work of Tsiolkovsky. They found, to their amazement and dismay, that the German was gaining worldwide recognition for rocket ideas that a Russian had originated two decades earlier.

Renewed publicity on the subject also prompted the Soviet military to consider ways to use rockets for military purposes. In the late 1920s the army's chief of armaments, Mikhail Tukhachevsky, began investigating two possibilities: hurling long-range explosives on enemy targets and as a means of getting aircraft launched more quickly with the shortest

Hermann Oberth reached the same conclusion as Tsiolkovsky and Goddard, that modern liquid fuels would be more powerful than powder.

problems since 1924. With the help of the amateurs, the Soviets constructed a rocket that reached a height of thirteen hundred feet in 1933.

GERMANY UPS THE ANTE

Meanwhile, Oberth's book created such a stir in his home country that the German military could not ignore it. They became especially intrigued with rockets because of restrictions placed on them by the Treaty of Versailles that concluded World War I. This treaty severely limited the numbers of heavy artillery pieces the Germans could produce, but it said nothing about rocket-powered weapons.

Germans such as Colonel Karl Becker, who envisioned a future war in which Germany reclaimed its honor, saw the same military advantages to rockets that the Soviets had noted. In 1929 Becker persuaded the ministry of defense to authorize a small program to study the feasibility of developing military rockets. Like the Soviets, the military relied on unpaid amateurs to do much of the research.

In 1930 the ministry of defense saw enough potential in rockets to assign engineer Walter Dornberger to supervise the rocket program. In May 1931, with most of the work still being done by amateurs, the Germans tested a liquid fuel rocket. Although they had no control at all over its direction, the rocket did soar a few thousand feet. The mixed result was enough to encourage the military, while

runway possible. His fledgling liquid rocket program achieved some success in 1929, when army staff engineer Valentin Glushko built an engine capable of achieving forty-four pounds of thrust by burning gasoline with liquid oxygen.

But progress was slow; the Soviets' combined effort still lagged well behind the work of the U.S. rocket expert, Robert Goddard, operating on his own. In an effort to speed up results, Tukhachevsky enlisted the aid of amateur rocket enthusiasts. In the early 1930s, he was able to obtain funding for the Society for the Study of Interplanetary Communications, a club whose members had been wrestling with rocket increasing the skepticism of Germany's political leaders.

Von Braun Arrives

In August 1932 the Germans recruited a twenty-year-old scientific prodigy to a civil service position with the army in the rocket development program. Wernher von Braun, the son of a prominent Prussian baron, had been intrigued at an early age by his mother's hobby of astronomy. During his youth he had eagerly read the works of Verne, Wells, and Oberth, which sparked a burning desire to build a spaceship that could take him to the moon. Educated in Swiss schools, von Braun earned a reputation as an engineering genius. To his father's disgust, he continued to focus his attention on the dream of space travel. He was thrilled when the German government offered him a chance to build rockets, which he saw as the vehicles of space travel.

Working long hours, von Braun quickly rose to the position of technical director of the rocket project. On December 31, 1932, he eagerly ignited his first test rocket, only to watch it explode on the launchpad. The failure stunned and discouraged von Braun. "It took us exactly a half year to build and one-half second to blow up,"[4] he noted.

German scientist Wernher von Braun (seen here in 1960) was thrilled when given the chance to build rockets by the German government.

Walter Dornberger, von Braun's superior who eventually attained the rank of general in the German army, encouraged him to take the defeat in stride. Dornberger knew from painful experience—a powder explosion that scarred his face and nearly killed him early in 1932—that rocket science was a risky business that could be advanced only by trial and error. "Don't worry, Wernher," comforted Dornberger. "We will have many failures, but from each we will learn."[5]

SECRETS AND SPIES

Von Braun took Dornberger's advice to heart and renewed his efforts. By 1934 his redesigned A-2 rocket soared to a height of nearly a mile. The project progressed so well that, two years later, the German military set up a new, tightly guarded research center at Peenemünde along the Baltic Sea for von Braun to carry out his experiments far from the prying eyes of potential enemies.

Von Braun and his team slowly developed methods of rocket guidance that were far superior to anything Goddard had made. Their autopilot technology was so revolutionary, involving mind-numbingly complex equations, that it took several years for the Germans to design and build laboratories in which their new ideas could be tested. As Dornberger had predicted, failures were frequent. Von Braun's initial experiments with his advanced A-3 rocket in 1937 ended in disaster.

Yet he and his staff sifted through the ashes of each failure to glean important information by which to construct the next rocket. Their first success came with a rocket-assisted aircraft in April 1937. While cruising at twenty-six hundred feet, test pilot Erich Warsitz ignited a rocket booster that shot him forward so quickly that he felt as though he had been "kicked in the backside."[6]

By 1939 the Germans were well on their way to developing the A-3 rocket, which—at 46 feet in length, 65 inches in diameter, and 27,000 pounds in weight—dwarfed anything that either Goddard or the Russians had attempted. With the capability of producing 56,000 pounds of thrust, it could carry an explosive device of 2,200 pounds with some degree of accuracy over a short distance.

THREAT OR DECOY?

In 1939 Germany invaded Poland, thus triggering World War II. At that time the rest of the world was completely unaware of the German rocket program. On October 17, 1939, the British embassy in Oslo, Norway, received a mysterious message offering information about Germany's secret weapons development program. Amid skepticism that this was a German decoy to set British intelligence on a wild-goose chase, the British signaled their interest.

On November 4 an embassy guard found a package on a ledge, addressed to Admiral Hector Boyles. Enclosed were eight pages of detailed information on new weapons including long-range rockets being developed at a secret site in

Peenemünde. Most British scientists, unaware of the breakthroughs made by von Braun and others, dismissed the idea of such weapons as ridiculous. They had looked into the possibility of rocket-based weapons years ago and had concluded that they would not work.

Their disdain for rocket weapons was hardly surprising; even the German high command, which had firsthand knowledge of von Braun's progress, showed little enthusiasm for the project. With the war going so well for his country in 1940, following the defeat of France, German leader Adolf Hitler decided that there was no point in wasting resources on unproven technology. Convinced that he could defeat the last remaining British forces on the European continent with conventional weapons, Hitler withdrew support from the rocket program.

THE A-4

German army officials, however, were not willing to let a potential military advantage go to waste. General Walther von Brauchitsch secretly authorized the assignment of five thousand specialists and technicians to Peenemünde to continue work on the rocket project. Slave labor from the prison camps was imported to expand the research area.

On June 13, 1942, the A-4—an ultrafast rocket with an accurate range of 160 miles—was ready for testing. Germany's minister for armaments, Albert Speer, stood by von Braun as the rocket was ignited. Technically, the test was another disappointment. The guidance system failed, which caused the rocket to fall to earth a half mile from the launch site. But the thunderous power of the liftoff so overwhelmed Speer that he became one of von Braun's chief supporters.

Von Braun desperately needed such support in high places. His rocket program faced stiff competition from other military branches for government funds. Even with Speer's support, von Braun realized he had to come up with a major success, and soon, to keep his project alive. The breakthrough came on October 13, 1942, when an A-4 roared off the launchpad and shattered the speed of sound. Streaking through the air at 3,500 miles per hour, the rocket soared 35 miles into the air and traveled 120 miles out into the sea. Von Braun had some anxious moments over the next six months as only one of the next eleven shots duplicated the success of October 13. But by the spring of 1943, the Peenemünde team had refined their techniques so that they were able to consistently and accurately launch their rockets.

VON BRAUN IN DANGER

When the German air force failed to defeat Great Britain, Hitler belatedly gave high priority to the rocket project in the summer of 1943. At that critical juncture, von Braun experienced a devastating setback. The Allies, finally convinced that the German weapons development threat was real, set out to destroy it. After determining the location of the Peenemünde facilities, they unleashed a massive bombing attack in August 1943 that wiped out a large portion of the rocket facilities. At great risk to his own life, von Braun rushed amid the falling bombs to save important research documents and blueprints.

Several months later von Braun's passion for space travel caused another crisis. Informers told Heinrich Himmler's secret police that they had overheard von Braun saying that his main objective in building rockets was to create a means of traveling in space. In March 1944 Himmler accused

The A-4 rocket, launched successfully on October 13, 1942, was a breakthrough for von Braun's program. It shattered the speed of sound and soared thirty-five miles into the air.

SUCCESSFUL LAUNCH

German rocket scientist Ernst Stuhlinger described the first successful launch of the rocket that came to be known as the V-2, quoted in Countdown: A History of Space Flight *by T. A. Heppenheimer:*

"We felt the heat of the rocket on our faces as soon as the flames developed. The sound was tremendous. We didn't hear with the ears only, but with the whole body. It was as if the entire skin was an eardrum vibrating. The rocket rose, very evenly. It moved as though nothing else on earth existed. It gained speed while the flame grew longer. It went straight up; then it began to tilt over, again very evenly. It went out over the Baltic, still as if no other motion existed."

the rocket scientist of not wholeheartedly pursuing his patriotic duty of building weapons for Germany and arrested him for treason. Von Braun was barely saved from execution by the last-minute intervention of Speer. The incident not only shook von Braun to the core but also delayed work on improving the A-4.

VENGEANCE WEAPONS

Von Braun's A-4 rocket was renamed V-2, short for Vergeltungswaffe, or "Vengeance" weapon. These rockets flew so fast that there was no defense against them, and they could be launched from mobile sites. With German defenses collapsing against the Russians in the east, the Allies in the south, and a new Allied invasion from the west, the V-2 was Germany's last hope of turning the tide of the war.

On September 8, 1944, this weapon was finally ready for use against Great Britain. Von Braun supervised the firing of the first rocket. Still battling mixed emotions about how his invention was being used, von Braun privately grumbled, "It behaved perfectly but landed on the wrong planet."[7] His motive for building rockets had always been space travel.

The 3,225 V-2s fired against Great Britain showered destruction on its cities. The Allied air forces frantically stepped up their attacks on Peenemünde. In order to save their rocket program from Allied bombs, the Germans moved the entire operation far inland to the Hartz Mountains of central Germany. Over eleven thousand prisoners worked to carve out bombproof facilities in the mountains. Early in 1945 more than five thousand scientists and technicians made the dangerous caravan by truck from Peenemünde to the Hartz

Mountains under periodic strafing by Allied planes.

The V-2, however, had arrived too late to seriously affect the course of the war. German resistance was being crushed on all fronts. This put Germany in an unusual situation: the side with superior military technology was about to go down in defeat.

SOVIET ROCKET TECHNOLOGY AT WAR'S END

Germany's closest competitor in the rocket race, the Soviet Union, suffered even more than Germany from the paranoid state of its leaders. As part of a massive purge of suspected opponents, Soviet leader Joseph Stalin killed or imprisoned most of the top experts involved in rocket research. Among those arrested was Sergei Korolev.

Born in the Ukraine in 1906, Korolev's fascination with engineering and aviation had led him to enroll at the Bauman Higher Technology School in Moscow. While studying there, he learned of the pioneering work of Tsiolkovsky in theoretical spaceflight. The challenge of spaceflight captivated young Korolev. While working at an aviation design bureau in Moscow after graduation, he took an active role in one of the amateur rocket clubs working with the Soviet military. After one of the club's rockets reached a height of thirteen hundred feet in 1933, Korolev was invited to join a new organization called the Scientific Research Institution of Reaction Propulsion as assistant director.

For several years he struggled with the painful sequence of trial and error that was the lot of all early rocket researchers. His superiors, however, were not nearly as forgiving as Dornberger. In June 1938 Korolev was arrested and charged with impeding the progress of the nation's rocket studies. He was sentenced to ten years of hard labor at a mine in Siberia, a sentence that normally was equivalent to death. But after serving a few months, Korolev somehow got his case reopened. He eventually was allowed to return to Moscow as part of a group of skilled pris-

Sergei Korolev made great contributions to the Soviet Union's development of rocket technology.

oners working as virtual slaves for aircraft designers. Korolev and his fellow prisoners were instrumental in developing aircraft that helped turn back the German offensive into Russia. Later in the war, he received a transfer to his first love—a rocket design project.

Unknown to most of the world, the Soviet Union made remarkable progress in rocket-powered aircraft technology while Korolev and his comrades were on the project. Even before the Germans had perfected their rocket-powered Komet fighters, the Soviets produced a twenty-one-foot interceptor known as the BI. According to their engineer's calculations, the BI was capable of flying more than six hundred miles per hour. Test pilot Grigori Bakhchivandzhe took off in a BI on March 27, 1943, to check out the new plane. But after reaching speeds of over five hundred miles per hour, the plane plunged out of control and slammed into the earth, killing Bakhchivandzhe.

Subsequent wind tunnel tests confirmed that high speeds produced incredible stresses that made the plane unmanageable. Unsure of how to combat these stresses, and lacking the scientific expertise and the massive government backing of the German missile program, the Soviets abandoned their effort. That left only the United States as a potential rival to the German rocket program.

STATE OF U.S. ROCKET RESEARCH

The United States, however, lagged behind even the Russians. Other than God-

Members of the American Rocket Society work on an early model. Rocket research in the United States lagged behind programs in Russia and Germany.

dard, the only Americans working on rocket technology before the war were amateurs. The foremost of these was the American Rocket Society, founded in 1930. One member of this group, Princeton University graduate James Wyld, built a small, reliable rocket in 1941. Another club member, Lovell Lawrence, approached the U.S. government about building on Wyld's accomplishment. When informed that the government was forbidden by law from contracting with individuals, Lawrence set up a corporation called Reaction Motors, and in 1942 this corporation landed a government research contract. By the end of the war, Reaction Motors was able to produce a rocket with three thousand pounds of thrust—a respectable accomplishment but nowhere near what the Germans had accomplished.

Theodor von Kármán followed an almost identical path in advancing the cause of rocket science in the United States. While serving as professor of aeronautics at the California Institute of Technology (Caltech), the Hungarian-born von Kármán became intensely interested in rockets while helping a graduate student prepare for his doctoral dissertation on the subject. General Henry Arnold of the air force was one of the few American military leaders who saw the potential of rocket research for military uses. In the fall of 1938, Arnold called a meeting of an advisory committee on research and development and asked the members to choose from among his proposed projects. Jerome Hunsaker of the Massachusetts Institute of Technology opted to work on the problem of windshield deicing. Looking over at von Kármán, he expressed the common view of the U.S. scientific community toward rockets when he said, "Karman can take the Buck Rogers job."[8]

Von Kármán took the assignment and made enough progress constructing a reliable rocket engine that the navy grew interested in setting up a production facility to build the rockets. Since Caltech was unable to enter into such a commer-

cial venture, von Kármán and his associates set up companies that eventually grew into the Jet Propulsion Laboratory and Aerojet-General. Nonetheless, despite the heroic accomplishments of individual American rocket enthusiasts, the experts admitted that they were not even in the same league as the Germans. Von Kármán himself estimated that the United States would need twenty to twenty-five years to catch up to Germany in rocket science.

FATEFUL TIME

Holed up in their underground fortress during Germany's collapse in 1945, scientists like Dornberger and von Braun faced a precarious future. They were well aware they possessed valuable technology that their enemies would be pleased to obtain. Once the V-2s began raining down on London, the blinders had come off those military leaders around the world who had been scoffing at the idea of rocket research. The Germans had proved that the technology worked. At the very end of the war, von Braun and his staff were working on a multistage rocket powerful enough to fly across the Atlantic Ocean and hit New York or Washington. Although Germany's military position had deteriorated so badly that it was in no position to make good use of it, the advantage of being able to accurately lob explosives on an enemy from hundreds, or even thousands, of miles away became obvious. The United States, in particular, had an immediate interest in such mis-

To Whom Go the Spoils?

At a secret meeting of top scientists and engineers at a farmhouse near Peenemünde, Wernher von Braun raised the dilemma faced by German rocket scientists at the end of the war. This passage is quoted by William B. Breuer in Race to the Moon: America's Duel with the Soviets.

"Germany has lost the war. But let us not forget that it was our team that first succeeded in reaching outer space. We have never stopped believing in satellites, voyages to the moon and interplanetary travel. We have suffered many hardships due to our faith in the great peacetime future of the rocket. Now we have an obligation. Each of the conquerors will want our knowledge. The question we must answer is: to what country shall we entrust our heritage?"

siles in their continuing Pacific Ocean struggle against Japan. Furthermore, scientists throughout the world recognized that the rocket-building process was extremely complex and that their own research efforts could not begin to match what the Germans had accomplished.

But while their knowledge made von Braun and his associates valuable to their enemies, it put them in grave danger from their superiors. From past experience with Himmler, they feared that fanatical Nazi leaders might order them killed to prevent Germany's enemies from obtaining this knowledge.

The future of rocket research hinged on the fate of the German scientists and engineers. If they survived, they would tip the balance heavily in favor of whichever nation obtained their services. If von Braun and his associates were killed, their knowledge would die with them, and the race for rocket technology would start from scratch.

2 The U.S.-Soviet Missile Race

As the war drew to a close, it became obvious that the United States and the Soviet Union would emerge as the world's dominant powers. Although the two nations had joined together to defeat the Nazi menace, a gulf of distrust and intrigue lay between them. The Soviet Union was a communist state in which the government controlled the economy, and property was publicly, rather than privately, owned. It was philosophically opposed to the United States, which believed in relatively uncontrolled private ownership and free enterprise. Furthermore, the Soviet Union was run by a dictator, Joseph Stalin, while the United States believed in democratically elected officials.

Before the defeat of Germany was complete, the two allies were already jockeying for advantage in the postwar world. After suffering staggering losses in two world wars, the Soviet leadership was determined to safeguard its future by gaining a position of military strength. The government spent heavily to create the largest and most powerful army in the world. As this army rolled back the German forces from countries such as Poland and Czechoslovakia, it installed local communist governments loyal to the Soviet Union. The United States, dismayed by the brutal tactics of Soviet dictator Stalin, viewed with alarm the Soviets' strategy of aggressive expansion into Eastern Europe.

Mutual suspicion and fears of falling behind a potential enemy in missile technology drove members of both nations to gain as much German technology as they could before the other side did the same. When the Soviets captured a V-2 facility in Poland, Great Britain and the United States asked their Soviet allies to allow their technicians to inspect the site. Stalin agreed but did not let the technicians onto the site until the Soviets had dismantled and removed everything of value.

That ended any pretense of cooperation between the Soviets and the Western allies regarding German technology. In the spring of 1945, the United States had fourteen separate intelligence teams working in Germany, trying to beat their Soviet, French, and British counterparts to the treasure of German technological secrets.

DILEMMA OF THE GERMAN SCIENTISTS

As the Russians closed to within seventy-five miles of Peenemünde to the east and the Americans and British broke through Germany's borders on the west in 1945, Hitler ordered all scientific research and development facilities and documents destroyed. "If the war is lost, the nation will also perish," said Hitler. "It will be better to destroy things ourselves because this nation will have proved to be the weaker one and the future will belong solely to the stronger nations."[9]

Such orders horrified many German officials, some of whom did their best to ignore them. Even those who attempted to carry out the orders were not successful. At Bonn University, a Polish technician turned over to British and American forces some papers he had found partially flushed down a toilet. These papers contained a list of all German technological projects as well as the names of the scientists and technicians who worked on them. The list proved invaluable to Americans in locating and contacting key German personnel.

Meanwhile, German general Hans Kammler realized the war was over and feared that his enemies would exact revenge on him for his part in the war effort. To save his own skin, he selected five hundred research personnel, including von Braun, and ordered them to board a train

Soviet troops move forward against German defenses. As the Soviet army advanced, communist governments were installed in countries surrendered by the Germans.

heading south into the Bavarian Alps. His plan was to use the researchers as bargaining chips for lenient treatment from the Americans.

Von Braun found himself and his men confined to what amounted to a prison camp. Fortunately for him, Walter Dornberger managed to smuggle von Braun to a safe, secret location. Von Braun had come to believe that they would be better off cooperating with the Americans than with the Soviets. He had never abandoned his reason for being involved with rockets in the first place—the dream of traveling in space and visiting other planets. He estimated that the United States was the nation with the best chance of providing the financial and technical support he needed to make his long-standing dream of spaceflight possible.

Dornberger had independently come to the same conclusion. Their future lay with the Americans, if they could stay alive long enough to reach them. "The war is over," said Dornberger. "Now it is our obligation to place our baby [rocket research] in the right hands."[10]

AMERICANS HIT GOLD

On April 11, 1945, American troops in southern Germany discovered a railroad track leading straight into a mountain. Investigating further, they discovered the secret German V-2 assembly facilities, including components for a hundred of the long-range missiles. At about the same time, the Soviets suffered a discouraging setback. Their troops overran Peenemünde, only to find the missiles and scientists long gone and the facility 75 percent destroyed.

The American windfall continued three weeks later. Upon hearing that Hitler had committed suicide rather than surrender to the advancing Russian troops, von Braun's brother rode a bicycle down a mountain road until he came upon a U.S. military force. He told the startled soldiers that 150 top German scientists were hidden nearby and wished to offer their services to the Americans. U.S. intelligence soon discovered another 350 scientists and engineers scattered throughout the area under their control.

An American soldier examines a German V-2 component that was discovered in a secret assembly facility.

Recognizing the value of the missiles, the Americans made secret plans to spirit them back to the United States. But the high command was not certain what to do about the scientists. Many were highly suspicious of the Germans' motives in offering their services, especially when the newcomers did not act like a defeated enemy. The Germans expected something in return for their cooperation, including permission to bring their families to the United States. As von Braun said, "We were interested in continuing our work in the United States, not just being squeezed like a lemon [by the Americans] and discarded."[11] U.S. leaders also worried about public reaction to allowing the masterminds behind the terrible Nazi vengeance weapons to come to America.

TUG-OF-WAR

On May 7, 1945, Germany surrendered. While the Americans awaited clear orders as to what terms, if any, they could offer the German rocket experts, many of the Germans had second thoughts about joining them. Some drifted away back to their homes. Meanwhile the Soviets launched their own initiative to obtain German technology. They broadcast advertisements over Radio Berlin offering fat contracts and other perks to key German personnel.

By the end of May, the Americans were in danger of squandering all of their German rocket advantages. At a conference in Yalta, the Allied leaders had agreed to divide Germany into four spheres of influence. The area in which the Americans held the V-2 rockets and the scientists was assigned to the Soviets and was to be turned over to them by June 21. According to the agreement, nothing was to be moved out of the Soviet zone during the transition. This included tons of research documents, many of them related to rocket guidance control systems, which were recently discovered in a dynamited mine.

Major Robert Staver desperately cabled a complete report of the German rocket experts' situation to his superiors back home and strongly recommended offering them work in the United States. Staver's report finally touched a nerve, and he was given permission to smuggle out whom he could. Less than five hours before the Soviets were to take over the region, a train crammed with rocket experts and their families pulled out of the region.

The national security implications of rocket research were so high that even the United States and Great Britain abandoned their traditional close alliance in pursuit of the technology. The United States reneged on a pledge to give half the captured V-2s to Great Britain, while the British infuriated the United States by taking and holding Dornberger as a war prisoner.

THE SCIENTIST GRAB ESCALATES

On August 6 the United States intensified the scramble for German scientists when it dropped an atomic bomb on Hiroshima,

Japan. World leaders feared that such explosive devices could be incorporated into the new rocket technology to produce weapons that could be launched from thousands of miles away. With no defense against such weapons, their best recourse seemed to be in creating a standoff by producing an arsenal of nuclear ballistic missiles themselves that would deter the other side from using theirs.

With this incentive, Stalin redoubled his quest for German rocket expertise. He created a special intelligence committee under Georgy Malenkov to seek out and collect those German rocket experts who remained in Germany. At first the recruitment was voluntary. The promises of a large house and lavish benefits enticed Helmut Grotrupp, a high-ranking project manager at Peenemünde, to co-

The atomic bomb explodes over Hiroshima. World leaders feared that nuclear devices combined with rocket technology would produce powerful long-range weapons.

operate with the Soviets. Grotrupp had been one of those smuggled out of the Soviet zone by the Americans; but he had then experienced a change of heart. Some Germans, upset that the Americans were balking at their demands to bring their families with them to the United States, joined Grotrupp.

As the U.S. government continued to drag its feet in contract negotiations with von Braun and his team, who were still in Germany, American intelligence officials grew concerned that the Soviets would kidnap von Braun. Although this did not occur, in September 1945 the Soviets stepped up their campaign for German rocket science by demanding that all scientists, engineers, and technicians in their zone of influence register with the Soviet military. Scientists like Grotrupp, who had been lured by Soviet promises, began to worry about their personal freedom. These fears proved well founded when, on October 22, the Soviet military rounded up twenty-thousand Germans, including hundreds of missile technicians. All, including those like Grotrupp who had been promised lavish rewards, were forcibly transported to the Soviet Union to work as prisoners in rocket research facilities.

In the end, both the Americans and the Soviets each managed to narrowly avert disaster. The Soviets belatedly gathered just enough German expertise to allow them to compete with the Americans in the missile race. On the other hand, had Major Staver not managed, in the nick of time, to arouse interest back home for the German scientists, the Soviets could have walked off with rocket science expertise that would have put the United States at a huge disadvantage in the coming space race.

THE RISE OF THE GREAT DESIGNER

One of those assigned to obtain German rocket information was Sergei Korolev. Finally released from prisoner status in August 1944, Korolev did not let his harsh treatment at the hands of his own government erode his loyalty to the Soviet state. In 1945 he was commissioned into the Red Army and assigned to work on the Soviets' new long-range missile program.

Korolev went to Germany and put together his own research team from among the captured German experts, whom he moved to the new rocket research center near Moscow. There the German transplants found much of their old equipment and facilities, which the Russians had begun stripping and carting off from German production facilities even before the end of the war.

Rather than relying on the Germans to run the program and duplicate the success they had achieved at Peenemünde, Korolev used them only as resources. He extracted every bit of knowledge he could from them and then transferred that knowledge to his rocket projects, run by his own team of Soviet technicians. Before long Korolev had so mastered the principles of rocketry that he dominated the Soviet long-range missile program. He became such a valuable asset to the Soviet

WALLACE'S ADVICE

Secretary of Commerce Henry Wallace, who had previously served as Franklin Roosevelt's vice president, was one of the first high-level U.S. officials to recognize the value of the German scientists. He revealed his thoughts to President Truman in this December 4, 1945, letter, quoted in William B. Breuer's Race to the Moon: America's Duel with the Soviets.

"The transfer of outstanding German scientists to this country for the advancement of our science seems wise and logical. Presently under our control (in Germany) are eminent scientists whose contributions, if added to our own, would advance the frontiers of scientific knowledge for national benefit.

Many of the German scientists have already been transported to Russia . . . where their past and future knowledge will be incorporated in the scientific endeavors of that nation. . . . It is evident that many of the outstanding German scientists will no longer be available unless a decision is made quickly to permit their importation to this country."

military that they erased his name and background from all references, lest their enemies discover who he was and try to capture him. For more than a decade and a half, Korolev remained hidden from public view, known only as the Great Designer.

GERMAN ROCKET SCIENTISTS IN THE UNITED STATES

Meanwhile, Operation Overcast, the secret plan to bring German scientists to the United States, provoked intense opposition within the U.S. government. Fierce debate raged behind closed doors for months over the appropriateness of welcoming Nazi rocket scientists into the country. Secretary of Commerce Henry Wallace argued strongly that the government had a national security obligation to carry through with its plan to employ the Germans. Vannevar Bush—director of the Office of Scientific Research and Development and one of the most influential men in the creation of the computer—was just as insistent that bringing in Germans was foolish, arguing that American scientists could carry out any research required in rocket development.

While the debate continued, von Braun and his team secretly arrived at Fort Bliss, Texas, in September 1945 and set to work organizing the tons of captured documents. Another fifty-five scientists arrived in November, disguised as truck drivers.

The Truman administration hedged on its commitment to the Germans at first, offering them only six months of employment before they were to be sent back home. Before the time was up, however, the expertise and trustworthiness of the rocket scientists so impressed U.S. officials that over four hundred German rocket experts were retained on a permanent basis and their families were allowed to join them.

Under von Braun's direction, the U.S. research team assembled the captured V-2 rockets and test-fired one at the military's new missile testing range in the White Sands desert of New Mexico on June 28, 1946. The launch was a success as the rocket soared sixty-seven miles into space. U.S. officials conceded that the cooperation of von Braun and his staff saved the country ten years and $75 million of research. The hiring of von Braun was one of the greatest bargains in U.S. history. The rocket genius worked twelve to fourteen hours a day for several decades, never earning more then $10,000 a year for his efforts.

SEESAW BATTLE FOR SUPREMACY

In the postwar years, the United States secured a seemingly unassailable position as the dominant military power in the world. This was primarily due to the fact that they were the sole possessors of the horrific atomic bomb. But, thanks to von Braun, they also took the lead in rocket development. The United States then further demonstrated its superiority in aerospace technology in October 1947, when Chuck Yeager flew in an X-1 rocket-powered aircraft, a joint project of the army, Bell Aircraft, and Reaction Motors. Prior to this time, dozens of pilots throughout the world had died trying to break the sound barrier in a piloted aircraft. Yeager fired up all four rockets in the X-1's engine, which kicked in six thousand pounds of thrust and blasted the aircraft through that previously unbreakable barrier.

The Soviets, however, quickly responded to American successes. By the end of the decade, they succeeded in exploding their own atomic bomb. Meanwhile their government launched an all-out crusade to erase the gap in missile technology. A dictatorship has the advantage of decisive action while democracies must debate and vote, and Stalin used that advantage to the limit in rocket research. He provided whatever funds and workers his researchers required to get the job done. Led by Korolev, the Soviets made astounding progress. On October 30, 1947, little more than a year after von Braun's successful V-2 test, the Soviets fired their own V-2 rocket. The results of the test were chilling to the Americans. Not only did the launch fire perfectly, the rocket landed directly on a target 185 miles away.

Congress, frightened by news of the Soviet's successful atom bomb test in August 1949, appropriated $75 million to construct a rocket firing range at a remote location on the Florida coast known as Cape Canaveral. The former Redstone

Chuck Yeager stands next to an X-1 rocket-powered aircraft. In it, Yeager was the first pilot to break the sound barrier.

Arsenal in Huntsville, Alabama, which had produced military weapons for World War II, was converted to a rocket research center under the direction of von Braun.

The Cold War, as the continuing yet undeclared hostility between the United States and Soviet Union became known, produced a relentless quest for better and more powerful missiles. The range of missiles steadily increased until both sides began developing intercontinental ballistic missiles (ICBMs) that could accurately deliver a nuclear warhead on their enemy from a continent away.

Although the United States had far more material and industrial resources than the Soviets, their rival began to pull ahead in rocket power. While the Soviets pushed ahead with their massive program, the United States got bogged down in squabbling over which of the three main branches of the U.S. military was best qualified to conduct missile research and development. Instead of pooling their resources, all three carried out their own missile programs—the army with von Braun directing its Redstone project; the navy with its Vanguard program, and the air force with the Atlas project.

Virtually all of the rocket research and development on both sides took place in secret. In late 1952 *Time* magazine reported, "The Cold War has thrown a blackout over all rocket research. . . . Not one man on earth who knows the latest developments can talk freely about them."[12]

THE COLD WAR MOVES INTO SPACE

In the United States, von Braun faced the same tightrope-walking feat he had been forced to perform in Germany. From the start of his career, his only interest in rockets was as a vehicle for space exploration. The Nazis, however, had been interested in rockets solely for their use as weapons. In order to get backing for his work, von Braun had no choice but to develop the rockets for military applications. He had to suppress his enthusiasm for space travel in order to avoid execution by fanatical Nazi leaders.

Once the war was over, von Braun had allowed himself to again indulge in his dream. While recuperating from a serious bout of hepatitis shortly after joining the Americans, he had spent his time calculating the requirements of a rocket ship traveling to Mars, including the logistics of refueling at a halfway station. He had even allowed for the weight of a truck that the explorers would use to drive on the surface of Mars.

ROUSING THEIR SUPERIORS

In History of Rocketry and Space Travel *by Wernher von Braun and Frederick Ordway II, U.S. counterintelligence agent Charles Stewart described the difficulties he and others faced in getting their superiors to act regarding the German scientists:*

"When Dr. von Braun came out with General Dornberger and Colonel Axter, they lodged with us while we communicated with higher headquarters. None of us had scientific backgrounds, but the magnitude of their discoveries and their potential for the future was immediately apparent. We were dismayed when we could not arouse any interest in them at higher headquarters. Our first instructions were that they were to be thoroughly screened. . . . Our reply was to the effect that it made no difference if all were brothers of Hitler, because their unique knowledge made them extremely valuable militarily and from a national standpoint. After a few days, we were able to arrange their transfer to higher headquarters."

In the United States, von Braun found support from the scientific community for rocket development. His first V-2 rocket launched in 1946 carried a number of instruments to measure conditions in the upper atmosphere. Subsequent V-2s carried cameras and radiation detectors to record conditions a hundred miles from the surface of the earth. These were followed by experiments to test the effects of the upper atmosphere on living creatures, beginning with a colony of fruit flies packed onto one flight. On June 11, 1948, the United States sent a monkey on a thirty-nine-mile ride into the sky to test its reaction to the conditions.

Yet von Braun understood that there was a limit to what the United States would spend in the interests of science, let alone a far-fetched idea like space travel.

In order to maintain the backing for his rocket projects, he tried to convince the government that all of his rocket research, even his space exploration ideas, had sound practical applications. Once again von Braun, in order to promote his space ideas, pushed the envelope on military technology. He carried this over to the Cold War with the Soviets into outer space by stressing the potential military uses of satellites both for surveillance and for delivering weapons.

Von Braun's attempt to piggyback space exploration on military rocket development was never more apparent than in the early 1950s. In 1951 he produced a technical paper detailing his plan for a manned rocket mission to Mars. The following year he proposed a program to build and launch a perma-

To promote U.S. government interest in his rocket projects, von Braun stressed the potential military uses of satellites.

nent space station. Manned spaceflight, he insisted, "is as sure as the rising of the sun."[13] At the same time, he called for a massive U.S. commitment to beating the Soviets in space technology, warning that the nation's national security was at stake.

His critics regarded his military warnings as a blatant trick. "He is still thinking of space flight, not weapons, and he is trying to sell the U.S. a space flight project disguised as a means of dominating the world,"[14] fumed one. Von Braun's pleas for the massive space program were ignored.

The Soviets, meanwhile, detected a national interest in space quite apart from any military applications. Ever since the end of World War II, the Soviets had been trying to export their communist philosophy of government to Third World countries. Part of this process was a relentless propaganda campaign extolling the virtues and successes of communism. In the early 1950s, the Soviets determined that space exploration was an ideal forum for proving the superiority of their political system. Dramatic breakthroughs in space would make the whole world sit up and take notice of Soviet technological prowess. The Soviets began to dream big.

Under the direction of Korolev, the Great Designer, the Soviets diverted a major portion of their research and development resources to space exploration. The space race had begun, and only one country had left the starting blocks.

3 The Satellite Race

Although a substantial number of government leaders, as well as the public, viewed space exploration as unrealistic and frivolous, serious scientists had been lobbying for satellite research and development in both the United States and the Soviet Union since the end of the war. In 1946 a Los Angeles public affairs advocacy group known as the RAND Corporation wrote a report entitled "Preliminary Design of an Experimental World-Circling Spaceship." Arguing that such a satellite would have uses for scientific purposes such as weather observation as well as military surveillance, the report concluded, "The achievement of a satellite craft by the U.S. would inflame the imagination of mankind; and would probably produce repercussions in the world comparable to the explosion of the atomic bomb."[15] The U.S. government, however, remained unconvinced of the value of such a program.

In June 1948 Mikhail Tikhonravov, a friend and associate of Korolev, tried to present a paper on human-made satellites to the Soviet Union's Academy of Rocket and Artillery Science. His presentation was initially denied by a Soviet general, who told him, "We cannot include your report. Nobody would understand; they would accuse me of getting involved in things we do not need to get involved in."[16] Only after relentless lobbying by his friends did officials grudgingly relent and allow Tikhonravov on the program.

In the early 1950s, von Braun again tried to persuade U.S. government officials to back a satellite effort. U.S. secretary of defense Charles Wilson demanded that he come up with an immediate military need for a satellite. When von Braun could not, Wilson flatly rejected the idea. During the escalation of the Korean War in the early 1950s, a frustrated von Braun found himself diverted into design of a more immediately practical medium-range missile.

DISMISSING THE SOVIET CHALLENGE

Having recognized the propaganda value of space technology, the Soviets stopped scoffing at the notion of satellites and space adventures. They began to dream big. In 1952 the Soviet magazine *Ogonek* made the stunning prediction that the Soviets would land a man on the moon within fifty years. When Tikhonravov produced a new paper outlining the details of a satellite program two years later, the Soviets gave him a serious hearing. On August 2, 1955, a top Soviet scientist, Leo Sedov, mentioned at an international meeting of scientists that the Russians expected to put a satellite into orbit in the near future.

Almost everyone in the United States considered this unfounded boasting. After all, the U.S. missile program was led by von Braun, widely considered the world's foremost rocket expert, and even it had not achieved the thrust needed to shoot a rocket into orbit. The challenge of building a large rocket was enormously

complex. As von Braun explained to the press, "A large guided missile system involves from 60 to 80,000 changes in the missile alone before its first flight."[17] Some of the calculations required to design proper engine parts took weeks to complete. In many cases even the best calculations were useless. The only sure way to advance rocket knowledge was by the time-consuming method of constructing a rocket, testing it, determining what went wrong when the test failed, and making the changes necessary to overcome the problems. Believing that the Russians lagged well behind the United States in general technology, the American scientific community refused to concede that the Soviets could have leapfrogged past the United States in rocket expertise.

"THE COLUMBUS OF SPACE"

Von Braun and the Germans had many critics in the United States including an unnamed missile expert who had this to say about the rocket scientist in an article in the December 8, 1952, issue of Time *magazine:*

"Look at this von Braun! He is the man who lost the war for Hitler. His V-2 was a great engineering achievement, but it had almost no effect and it drained German brains and material from practical weapons. Von Braun has always wanted to be the Columbus of space. He was thinking of space, not weapons, when he sold the V-2 to Hitler. He says so himself. He is still thinking of space flight, not weapons, and he is trying to sell the U.S. a space flight project disguised as a means of dominating the world."

THE NONMILITARY PRIORITY

With the end of the Korean War in 1953, von Braun renewed his focus on building a rocket powerful enough to launch a satellite. By June 1954 testing was going so well on his Redstone rocket that von Braun presented to the government his proposal to put the world's first human-made satellite into orbit. He set June 1956 as the target date for the successful conclusion of Project Orbiter.

But even as von Braun's program proceeded, President Dwight Eisenhower harbored serious doubts about it. A former general who had commanded all Al-lied forces in the massive D-day invasion of Normandy during World War II, Eisenhower was sensitive to international fears of U.S. military power. He sought to reassure the nations of the world that despite the conflicts of the Cold War, the United States was committed to peace. Eisenhower worried about international reaction to the United States sending a satellite to orbit the earth. Would even friendly nations object to a U.S. surveillance object passing over their territory several times a day? In order to allay these fears and possible objections, Eisenhower determined that if the United States launched a satellite, it would have

One of von Braun's Redstone rockets is readied for flight. Von Braun believed that his rockets would launch the world's first man-made satellite into orbit by June of 1956.

to be exclusively of scientific and not military value. Although von Braun was personally more interested in scientific aerospace research than in military applications, he carried the stigma of being the inventor of the V-2 weapons and his current rocket program was part of a weapon's development project for the U.S. Army. Eisenhower decided to look elsewhere for a less-threatening satellite venture.

While the president was reaching this conclusion, the National Science Foundation urged the nation to help celebrate a worldwide scientific effort known as the International Geophysical Year (IGY) in 1956. The goal of the IGY was for scientists throughout the world to set aside their political differences and pool their technical knowledge to gain a better understanding of the earth and its atmosphere. One of the projects recommended by the National Science Foundation for IGY was the launching of a satellite to gather scientific data.

This was exactly the type of satellite project that Eisenhower wanted. In 1955 his administration put von Braun's project on the back shelf in favor of a nonmilitary satellite launching. The work was to be performed not by von Braun's rocket experts, but by the Naval Research Laboratory, whose Project Vanguard rocket program was to operate closely with the National Academy of Sciences and the National Science Foundation.

The decision raised a protest from army officials, one of whom called it "an astonishing piece of stupidity."[18] The Vanguard program was nowhere near as advanced as

their Jupiter program (as the Redstone was renamed). In July 1955 Vanguard officials confirmed this by announcing that they were aiming for a satellite launch date of July 1, 1957. Von Braun bitterly complained that the decision to replace Jupiter with Vanguard set the United States back so far that it guaranteed the Soviets would be first to send up a satellite.

Eisenhower administration officials paid no attention to the criticism. When asked at a press conference whether he was concerned that the Soviets might win the race to launch a satellite, Secretary of Defense Wilson remarked, "I wouldn't care if they did."[19] The decision stood, and von Braun's only consolation was that he was able to persuade the government to continue funding his rocket program, although on a reduced level, as a backup in case Vanguard failed.

Von Braun Sandbagged

The Soviets owned several advantages over the United States in the pioneer days of space exploration. Unlike the Eisenhower administration, Soviet leadership *did* care about beating the other side to technological space achievements. They were able to advance more quickly because their government controlled all aspects of research and development, while the United States had to go through a long process of bidding out various equipment and technology needs to private industry. Most importantly, the Soviets kept a tight lid on their progress in the space race while the United States, living in a more

CIVILIAN FLAVOR

President Eisenhower remained unconcerned about the Soviets' advantage in space technology. In Countdown: A History of Space Flight, *T. A. Heppenheimer quotes historian Walter McDougall on why Eisenhower refused to let von Braun launch his satellite earlier.*

"Speed was not the primary consideration; in the end, assuring the strongest civilian flavor in the project was more important. The administration was advised of the propagandistic value of being first into space. Of all these critical policy areas, however, the last had the lowest priority. For there were two ways the legal path could be cleared for reconnaissance satellites. One was if the United States got away with an initial small satellite—and had no one object to it. The other way was if the Soviet Union launched first.

The second solution was less desirable, but it was not worth taking every measure to prevent."

open society, freely gave the press information on its launch schedules. When the United States announced that it planned to send up a satellite in July 1957, the Soviets could gauge how much time they had to beat their rival to the punch.

In contrast, the United States had little idea of what the Soviet Union was doing. Reports from Soviet scientists at international professional meetings indicated that they had made astounding progress. Late in 1955 those scientists indicated that they knew how to build rockets with the necessary thrust and speed to launch a satellite. In 1956 U.S. intelligence determined that Soviet rockets were capable of launching missiles with reasonable accuracy at a range of fifteen hundred miles. Such reports alarmed Americans

to the point where the "missile gap" between the Soviets and the United States became a major campaign issue in the 1956 elections.

Still, neither side had yet demonstrated the technology required to launch a satellite. When Soviet scientists hinted that they were planning a satellite launch late in 1957, few Americans took them seriously.

One person who did was von Braun. He proceeded rapidly to perfect a four-stage rocket called the Jupiter C. Multistage rockets, although even more complicated than single-stage rockets, showed far more promise of delivering a load into orbit. A single-stage rocket required an enormous amount of fuel to get off the ground. There came a point where the weight of the fuel required to achieve a certain speed was so great that the rocket had to be impossibly huge to carry that weight. In a multistage launch, a large, heavy rocket engine could provide the initial burst off the ground. At a certain level, that stage would drop off and a second rocket would fire. This new thrust, combined with the existing speed of the rocket, could carry the much lighter second stage to greater speeds and heights than could a single-stage rocket on its own. Von Braun's Jupiter added third and fourth stages to increase the final stage's speed to 17,500 miles per hour—enough to allow a small object to escape the gravitational pull of the earth and go into orbit.

In 1956 von Braun put one of these rockets on the launchpad. His army superiors, however, were under orders to let the Vanguard project launch the nation's first satellite. Suspicious that von Braun planned to send up his own satellite, army brass ordered the fourth stage disabled and filled with sand to prevent it from "accidentally" being shot into orbit. The test firing was a success. On September 9, 1956, the Jupiter soared 682 miles into the air, reaching a top speed of sixteen thousand miles per hour. Had a satellite been mounted on the fourth stage instead of the sandbag, von Braun very likely could have launched it into orbit.

Meanwhile, Vanguard was progressing more slowly than expected. Von Braun, eager to step into the void, readied seven more Jupiter rockets, each capable of launching a satellite into orbit, and awaited word from the government to go ahead.

That word never came. While von Braun waited, the Vanguard program, under the direction of Dr. Milton Rosen, moved into the experimental stage. Test launches were made in December 1956 and May 1957. But neither launch showed the capability of sending a satellite into orbit. It was obvious that the program was not going to meet its July target.

KOROLEV'S DASH TO BE FIRST

In the Soviet Union, Korolev kept an anxious eye on the Americans' progress. Even more than his government, the Great Designer was obsessed with being first in space. Knowing that the United States was nearing the point of launching a satellite, he pressed ahead at a relentless pace.

Korolev's rocket program raced far ahead of the Soviet satellite effort. He had redesigned von Braun's V-2 into the R-7 rocket, whose primary function was to carry nuclear warheads, for the purpose of launching a satellite. With the satellite project still in the drawing stage, he had no idea how large the proposed satellite would be. He decided to leave plenty of margin for error by custom-building an R-7 large enough to launch an enormous satellite.

In 1956, while Korolev's rocket construction proceeded on schedule, the satellite designers fell far behind. Fearing that further delays would surrender the honor of the first satellite to the Americans, the Soviets finally scrapped plans for a high-tech satellite and settled for a

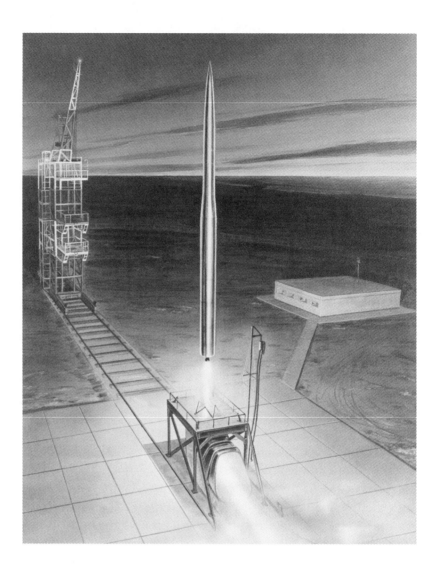

Pictured is an artist's conception of a Vanguard launch. Test flights did not show the rocket capable of carrying a satellite into orbit.

simple aluminum sphere. Designated the PS-1—short for Prostreishiy Sputnik, or "Simple Satellite"—the satellite was 22.5 inches in diameter, weighed 184 pounds, and had little function. The only scientific instruments aboard were a detector to measure electron concentration in outer space and a crude battery-operated radio transmitter.

Ever aware of the historical significance of what he was doing, Korolev insisted that the satellite's shiny surface be polished to perfection. "This ball will be exhibited in museums,"[20] he noted.

During the late summer of 1957, Korolev got a scare when he read the agenda for a meeting of the Congress of the International Astronautical Federation. The Soviet timetable called for the satellite launching to take place on October 6. Korolev saw that U.S. scientists were scheduled to present a symposium at the conference on that very date, entitled "Satellite over the Planet." Korolev could imagine only one reason for such a presentation: to announce the success of a satellite launching, probably on the previous day. To make sure that he beat the Americans, he moved the launch date up two days to October 4.

The launch took place as scheduled and proved a remarkable success. *Sputnik*, as the Soviet press dubbed the satellite, broke through the gravitational pull and began circling the earth at an altitude of 560 miles. It completed an orbit of the earth every hour and thirty-five seconds, emitting curious chirps over the radio to listeners below.

The Soviet government wasted no time in taking advantage of the propaganda victory it had sought and won. "The present generation will witness how the freed and conscious labor of the people of the new socialist society turns the most daring of man's dreams into reality,"[21] crowed the Soviet press.

The National Broadcasting Company announced the Soviet's triumph over a

Highly polished in recognition of its historical significance, Sputnik *nevertheless did little more than measure electron concentration in outer space.*

background of blips coming from *Sputnik*. "Listen now for the sound which forever more separates the old from the new,"[22] said the announcer.

U.S. REACTION TO *SPUTNIK*

The success of *Sputnik* took the United States by surprise. U.S. intelligence had uncovered no indication that such a launching was in the works. On October 3 the American people had gone to bed secure in the belief that their nation was the most powerful, technologically advanced country in the world. They awoke to find that the Soviets' success with *Sputnik* called that assumption into question. Now the United States's archenemy not only owned a terrifying nuclear arsenal but had capability that the United States lacked to send equipment orbiting over the planet— over the heads of U.S. citizens.

President Eisenhower, noting that *Sputnik* did not actually perform any significant task, shrugged off the Soviets' accomplishment. Although somewhat bothered by the military consequences of the Soviets' having taken an obvious lead in missile technology, he insisted, "So far as the satellite itself is concerned, that does not raise my apprehension, not one iota."[23] In fact, *Sputnik* fell out of orbit and plummeted back to earth in a few months.

In a way, the *Sputnik* launching was actually a relief to Eisenhower. Now that the Soviets had taken the first step of sending a satellite circling the earth and had drawn no protest, the United States no

longer had to worry about world reaction to its satellite efforts. Vanguard and other space programs, including von Braun's, could now proceed full speed.

Other Americans took the news far less calmly. Many major newspapers reacted with alarm and severely criticized the nation's leadership for allowing the Soviets to win the satellite race. Washington senator Henry Jackson proclaimed "a week of shame and danger"[24] for the nation. Trevor Gardner, former assistant secretary of the air force for research and development, blamed the wasteful duplication of effort among the armed forces for losing America's missile technology lead. "We have presently at least nine [rocket] programs," Gardner pointed out, "all competing for roughly the same kind of facilities, the same kind of brains, the same kind of engines and the same public attention."[25]

The furor was particularly galling to von Braun and his staff. He knew full well that his Jupiter rocket could have launched its own satellite a full year before the Soviets, had the U.S. government allowed it. But making that argument in the face of the Soviet triumph would only sound like sour grapes to the public, and so von Braun had to endure scathing criticism while his counterpart in the Soviet Union basked in glory.

SOVIET TRIUMPH, U.S. HUMILIATION

While Americans were still wringing their hands over losing the satellite race, Ko-

A GRIM AND TIMELY REMINDER

Vice President Richard Nixon tried to find a balance between President Eisenhower's apparent nonchalance over the Soviets' Sputnik *triumph and the public's handwringing. In an address quoted by* Time *in its October 14, 1957, issue, Nixon said:*

"Militarily the Soviet Union is not one bit stronger today than it was before the satellite was launched. The free world remains militarily stronger than the Communist world. . . . But at the same time we could make no greater mistake than to brush off this event as a scientific stunt of more significance to the man on the moon than to men on earth. We have a grim and timely reminder that we must never overlook—that the Soviet Union has developed a scientific and industrial capacity of great magnitude. The launch of the satellite will have rendered a signal service to the cause of freedom if only we react strongly and intelligently to its implications."

rolev dealt his archrivals an even more stunning blow. On November 2, less than a month after *Sputnik* was launched, Korolev fired an even larger satellite into orbit. This launching hammered home the overwhelming Soviet advantage in rockets by hurling a satellite weighing 1,120 pounds into the air, at a time when the American Vanguard program still had not figured out how to harness enough power to put anything into orbit. To make matters worse, *Sputnik 2* was far more than a shiny chunk of metal. It carried history's first space traveler, a dog named Laika, that was hooked up to various scientific instruments to measure the effects of space travel on living things. Laika's heartbeat increased rapidly during the ascent, but once the satellite settled into orbit, returned to normal. The dog survived comfortably for a hundred hours until the satellite's oxygen supply began to run out, and the dog was painlessly put to death by remote control. This was the first evidence that living creatures, and perhaps humans, could survive the stress of space travel.

This remarkable and totally unexpected Soviet accomplishment put enormous pressure on the United States to get into the space race, and quickly. Although John P. Hagen, director of the Vanguard program, insisted, "We are not attempting in any way to race with the Russians,"[26] the American public desperately looked to their government to do something to salvage U.S. pride and confidence. This pressure caused the United States to advance the next Vanguard rocket launching, scheduled for early 1958, to December 4.

Interest in the space program grew so intense that, on that date, the remote Cape Canaveral launch area was swarming with crowds eager to witness America's answer to the Soviet challenge. In reality, the goal of the Vanguard mission was laughably modest. The navy did not originally intend it as a satellite launching but rather as a test of their rocket. In comparison with the half-ton life-support system that the Soviets had hurled into space, the navy's T-3 three-stage rocket carried only a puny 3.25-pound, basketball-sized satellite.

While the crowds waited impatiently, the launch was delayed for two days, first by a frozen valve and then by high winds. But finally, on December 6, 1957, before an anxious audience, launch directors fired the ignition button. The launchpad rumbled as the rocket engines lit. With flames spewing from its bottom, the rocket lifted off the ground. The exhilaration of the onlookers, however, quickly deflated as the rocket dropped and toppled over. The rocket and the launchpad exploded in a cloud of fire and smoke.

The Vanguard rocket explodes on the pad on December 6, 1957. The failure was a major propaganda victory for the Soviets.

ADVANTAGE OF SECRECY

The spectacular public failure of the Vanguard launching in the face of such high expectations and media hype provided a major propaganda advantage for the Soviets in the space race: an aura of invincibility compared to the perceived bungling of the Americans.

This perception arose because rocket building remained an extremely complex process that relied heavily on trial and error to point the way to future improvements. Failures were an expected part of the process. In the United States, those failures took place in full view, provoking ridicule and accusations of incompetence from an impatient public. This was especially true of the ill-fated Vanguard program. The program's effort to redeem itself with a new launching in January had to be placed on hold when a second-stage engine proved faulty and needed to be replaced. The flight was moved back to February 5, 1958, and this time the control system failed before the satellite could be placed into orbit.

The Soviets, meanwhile, shielded their failures from the public. No one beyond a closed circle of scientists and technicians knew when the Soviets were launching a rocket. The Soviets reported only their successes and managed to keep their failures hidden for decades. While the Vanguard was subjected to agonizing public humiliation, the Soviets' third satellite shot, on February 3, 1958, failed when the rocket inexplicably lost power. Since the launch was done in secret, the failure was never witnessed or reported by outside sources. Observers, seeing only an unbroken string of Soviet triumphs on one hand and repeated American disasters on the other, concluded that the Soviets' superiority was overwhelming.

SATELLITE SUCCESSES AND FAILURES

With the Vanguard program publicly floundering, the government finally decided to let von Braun take his shot at a satellite launching. Jet Propulsion Laboratory (JPL) was assigned the task of rushing into production a functional satellite. In a little over two months, they designed and built a bullet-shaped, thirty-pound satellite dubbed the *Explorer 1*, which contained eighteen pounds of scientific measuring instruments.

The satellite launch was scheduled for January 29, 1958, but again the fates seemed to be conspiring against the Americans. High winds in the upper atmosphere forced the flight to be postponed. Finally, late at night on January 31, 1958, the Jupiter C rocket carrying the *Explorer 1* roared off into space. The launch appeared to go well, but the project directors did not know for sure if the satellite was in orbit until it emerged from the other side of the earth. Ninety minutes later, the time the satellite was calculated to appear, all was ominously quiet. Just when the Americans were contemplating yet another setback, a San Diego radar picked up the *Explorer*'s signal. The delay had occurred because the satellite had reached a higher, and therefore longer, orbit than planned.

Von Braun (right) and two colleagues hold up Explorer 1, *the first satellite that would be successfully launched by the Americans.*

A few weeks later, von Braun summed up the significance of the event. "With Explorer, we made a modest beginning," he said. "We have stepped into a new, high road, from which there can be no turning back."[27]

That road continued to be riddled with potholes, both for the United States and the Soviet Union. Vanguard suffered another humiliating launchpad explosion in February. Von Braun's follow-up attempt on March 5 failed when the fourth stage of his rocket did not ignite, causing the *Explorer 2* satellite to crash to earth. On March 17 the long-suffering Vanguard program finally achieved success, sending into orbit a three-pound satellite, equipped with photo cells capable of transmitting blurry pictures of cloud cover. Eleven days later von Braun successfully launched his second satellite. But at the end of April, another Vanguard rocket launching failed. At the end of May, two weeks after the Soviets announced the launching of the enormous *Sputnik 3*, weighing nearly one and a half tons, yet another Vanguard rocket lost power in the third stage and dropped its satellite into the ocean.

In an attempt to crush the American spirit by stretching its already large space technology lead to spectacular lengths, Korolev fit a spaceship weighing over eight hundred pounds atop an R-7 rocket and took aim at the moon. The rocket, however, lost power almost immediately after ignition on June 25, and the Soviets'

bold stab at reaching the moon went unnoticed. The very next day, another Vanguard rocket plunged into the ocean after a second-stage failure, an event that was well covered and ridiculed by the press.

BIRTH OF NASA

Eisenhower considered the public hysteria over the Soviets' space accomplishments to be foolish, and he insisted he had no intention of "getting involved in a pathetic race."[28] He insisted that while the Soviets

On March 17, 1958, Vanguard was launched into orbit. Seen here is the satellite with its photo cells that would later transmit pictures of cloud cover.

were collecting the glory with their dramatic stunts, the United States was actually collecting more valuable scientific data. Indeed, U.S. satellites equipped with cosmic ray detectors discovered vast concentrations of radiation about the earth that came to be known as Van Allen radiation belts. During 1958 and 1959, the United States successfully launched a total of eighteen satellites compared to only four by the Soviets. Later the United States would quietly earn far less publicized firsts in space, such as the first weather satellite in 1960 and the first television satellite in 1962. Furthermore, while all Sputniks soon crashed to earth, the *Explorer 1* continued to circle the earth until 1970, while the first Vanguard satellite remains in orbit to this day.

Nonetheless, the political climate of the times demanded that Eisenhower take action to reassure the American people that the United States was not lapsing into a second-rate power. Eisenhower continued to resist the idea of ceding space exploration to the military. Therefore, instead of putting von Braun and the army in charge of the U.S. space program, he took the advice of Vice President Richard Nixon and asked Congress to create a new civilian agency. Congress agreed, and on October 1, 1958, Eisenhower signed a bill creating the National Aeronautics and Space Administration (NASA).

NASA absorbed the eight thousand employees of the National Advisory Committee on Aeronautics along with those involved in the Vanguard programs, plus military resources such as von Braun's army rocket researchers and eventually the army-owned JPL. NASA proved to be an important step in laying the foundation for a U.S. challenge to Soviet space superiority.

Chapter

4 The Race for Manned Spaceflight

Once the principles of satellite launching and orbiting had been established, the next event in the race for space glory was sending humans into space. U.S. intelligence officials concluded that the sheer size of *Sputnik 3* was an indication that this feat was next on the Soviets' agenda.

While U.S. space experts urged the nation to undertake a massive attempt to beat the Soviets to that goal, Eisenhower would have none of it. One of his main priorities was cutting government spending, and even the most optimistic projections conceded that putting a person in space would cost billions.

Nor was much of the U.S. scientific and engineering community behind the effort. The space program was commonly viewed as a frivolous, impractical exercise of no lasting value. Those who joined NASA did so at their own risk and against the advice of colleagues. One professional considering a move to NASA was told, "You don't want to ruin your career. There's nothing going to come of this, and you're going to be hurt by it."[29]

NASA did catch two breaks in its first days of operation. First, Bob Gilruth signed on to lead the NASA space program. A Minnesotan who had worked on test data for transonic speeds since the 1940s, Gilruth proved a remarkably able and innovative project director. While Korolev charged forward to achieve historic firsts as quickly as possible, Gilruth steadily laid the foundation for an efficient long-range program.

Secondly, a new Canadian government was voted into office. On January 20, 1959, it decided to cancel research and development on the world's most advanced fighter aircraft, the Arrow, which was designed to fly at three times the speed of sound. The Canadian corporation working on the project, A.V. Roe, suddenly had no need for more than fourteen thousand employees, many of whom were top aeronautics experts. NASA was able to attract the bulk of these unemployed experts, and they gave the U.S. space program a much needed shot of professionalism.

BRINGING IN THE ASTRONAUTS

Immediately upon its creation, NASA began planning for human space travel. Those who transferred from the National

NASA's program to send humans into space was not supported by President Eisenhower, who wanted to cut government spending.

Advisory Committee on Aeronautics had already considered the project for a few months and had wrestled with some key issues. Among the most important was finding a way to deal with the tremendous heat that a spaceship would produce at high speeds as it reentered the earth's atmosphere. The scientists and engineers solved the problem, in theory, by designing a blunt end equipped with a shield to deflect the heat. They realized they also needed a system of retro-rockets to align the capsule correctly for the descent, as well as a mechanism for detaching that shield before the parachutes breaking the fall were deployed.

The next step was finding people to volunteer for space travel. In December 1958 NASA prepared to accept civil service applications for the position of astronaut. Ever cost-conscious, Eisenhower told them that this was ridiculous. The armed forces already had plenty of test pilots on the payroll, and the president ordered NASA to use them. In January 1959 NASA asked military commanders to nominate pilots for the position of astronaut. Eventually seven were chosen.

Projects Mercury and Vostok

By April 1959 NASA had a detailed plan to put an astronaut into spaceflight, a project known as Mercury. One key element of the project was the construction of a system of tracking stations around the world that could keep in continuous contact with spaceships as they orbited the earth. These stations would monitor such important factors as the position, speed, and direction of the spacecraft, environmental conditions aboard the craft, and direct communication with the astronauts. A group of corporations led by Bell Telephone undertook a crash program to erect eighteen tracking stations, including sites in Nigeria, the Canary Islands, Hawaii, and Mexico. Two of the stations were put on mobile ships. With more than thirty thousand workers on the job at once, the stations were completed in an astounding eighteen weeks.

The U.S. approach to space travel differed from Korolev's manned space program, known as Vostok, in two important ways. First, they had to cope with the fact that, as the Soviets proudly boasted, U.S. rockets were far less powerful than those

One of the most important parts of the Mercury program was the construction of tracking stations around the world that could keep in contact with orbiting spaceships.

of their rivals. The Mercury program had to compensate for its smaller rockets by being more concerned about the weight of the spacecraft components. For example, in order to contain the pressure of a normal atmosphere, a space capsule required a strong, heavy metal skin. For the Soviets, this was no problem. The Americans, however, had to cut weight from their craft; for the capsule atmosphere, they used pure oxygen, which required less pressure and could be contained by a thinner exterior. By necessity, the United States became far more adept than the Soviet Union at reducing the size of components. Eventually, U.S. experience with miniaturization would prove a great advantage as the United States was able to pack far more equipment on their spacecrafts.

Secondly, the U.S. space program depended on skilled astronauts to take an active part in designing and operating the spacecraft. As Gilruth told the seven astronauts, "We picked you fellows because you're test pilots. . . . Anytime you see anything, anytime you think something needs more testing, or even should be redesigned, I want you to let me know."[30]

This dependence on astronauts did not always sit well with engineers and technicians. At one planning meeting, an engineer from North American Rockwell complained, "We were on schedule and moving along just fine until the astronauts came out there and began working with us full-time. Now it's going slower and slower."[31] Gilruth did not care; if the men riding the rocket were not satisfied with the equipment, then

neither was he. Their expertise proved important from the start. No sooner did the astronauts see the first design of the Mercury capsule than they insisted that a window had to be added.

In contrast, Korolev was preoccupied with building flawless machines that he could design and program to do what he wanted. In his system, the cosmonauts (as the Soviets called their space pilots) were basically passengers along for a ride. The diminished importance of cosmonauts was evidenced by the fact that although the Soviets were well ahead of the United States in space technology, they did not begin training astronauts until more than a year after the United States started its program.

SHOOTING FOR THE MOON

Unknown to the public, while both the Soviets and Americans geared up for their race to put a human in space, they engaged in a secret competition to launch a rocket to the moon. Korolev made the first attempt in June 1958. The rocket failed to reach the necessary speed to break the earth's gravitational pull, however, and fell back to earth. In August a rocket carrying the U.S. attempt at a moon probe failed in the first stage. The United States made three more attempts. The closest it came to success was in October when *Pioneer 1* set a new altitude record of 70,746 miles before falling back.

Meanwhile Korolev failed in both of his next two attempts. On January 2, 1959, however, his *Lunik 1* finally succeeded in leaving the earth's influence and heading out into deep space. The Soviets had the spacecraft release a yellow cloud of sodium to make certain that astronomy observers throughout the world could see that their ship was leaving orbit. They also glossed over the fact that although they were trying to hit the moon, *Lunik*'s trajectory was so far off that it missed its target by over thirty-seven hundred miles. The United States claimed a small morale boost when, in March, their *Pioneer 4* broke free from the earth and hurtled toward the moon. However, it missed by even more than *Lunik 1*, sailing 37,300 miles off course.

Over the next eight months, Korolev and his team worked the glitches out of the trajectory and guidance system. On September 12, following a perfect launch, *Lunik 2* blasted into space and stayed perfectly on target. Three days later it struck the moon, giving the Soviets yet another space victory.

Korolev followed up this success with an even more spectacular triumph. On October 4 the Soviet Union launched *Lunik 3*, the most complex spacecraft yet devised. *Lunik 3* was equipped with in-flight control thrusters, solar-powered fuel cells, and had the hardware to respond to new commands from earth. It cleverly solved the problem of overheating (on the side of the capsule facing the sun) and brutal freezing (on the dark side) by continually rotating, like a barbecue spit.

Instead of slamming into the moon, *Lunik 3* went into orbit around it. Equipped with an automatic photo system that not only took pictures but removed the film from the camera, scanned it, and transmitted it back to earth, the spacecraft gave humans their first views of the dark side of the moon.

The rest of the world, unaware of the previous Soviet failures, hailed this latest achievement as yet another triumph of the apparently flawless Soviet space program.

"The first man in space? Most likely a Russian," lamented Edwin Diamond of *Newsweek*. "A mission to Mars? The Russians won't pass up the chance next year. The first man on the moon? He'll be carrying a hammer and sickle."[32]

MERCURY TEST FLIGHTS

NASA originally set January 1960 as the target date for the first manned suborbital spaceflight. But long before then, it was obvious that they would not come close to achieving their goal. Both the Atlas rocket and the Mercury capsule ran into a host of delaying problems. The first test of a booster rocket fizzled. It was not until October 9, 1959, that NASA achieved liftoff with an Atlas in a test of the heat shield and parachute system. Both worked, although the rocket failed to detach from the capsule as it should.

The astronauts had their own difficulties with the NASA physicians, who took a very cautious approach to their work. The doctors refused to clear the astronauts for flight until they had a better handle on the stresses the men would encounter. Centrifuge runs in which the astronauts were spun around at horrendous speeds provided some simulation data. Monkeys would provide the rest.

On May 28, 1959, two monkeys named Baker and Able were heavily wired and strapped into the nose of a Jupiter rocket.

These first American space riders flew 360 miles into the air and splashed down in the Atlantic Ocean after a trip of 1,700 miles, no worse for the experience. In December 1959 NASA performed its first test of the Mercury equipment by placing

AVOIDING THE SPACE RACE

In a speech delivered in 1960, Eisenhower's former science adviser Jack Killian made the case for avoiding a space race with the Soviets. This passage is quoted in The Decision to Go to the Moon *by John M. Logsdon.*

"The Soviets . . . have used technology as an instrument of propaganda and power politics, as illustrated by their great and successful efforts—and careful political timing—in space exploration. They have sought constantly to present spectacular accomplishments in space as an index of national strength. . . . But their expensive emphasis on space exploration will not be enough in the long pull to sustain an image of strength. This will be accomplished by a balanced effort in science and technology.

I believe that in space exploration, as in all other fields we choose to go into, we must never be content to be second best, but I do not believe that this requires us to engage in a prestige race with the Soviets. We should pursue our own objectives in space science, and not let the Soviets choose them for us by our copying what they do. In the long run we can weaken our science and technology and lower our international prestige by frantically indulging in unnecessary competition and prestige motivated projects. . . .

Unless decisions result in containing our development of man-in-space systems and big rockets boosters, we will soon have committed ourselves to a multibillion dollar space program. . . . Will several billion dollars a year additional for enhancing the quality of education do more for the future of the United States and its position in the world than several billion dollars additional for man-in-space?"

Sam, a rhesus monkey, into a Mercury capsule atop a rocket and launching him into space. High winds prevented the capsule from reaching its intended altitude of 400,000 feet, and it landed far short of its target. But Sam also survived the ride with no ill effects. Yet another monkey, named Miss Sam, went up in a rocket in late January 1960 and was trained to perform specific tasks during flight. Its inefficiency in performing these tasks during the test created doubts about whether astronauts could function under the stress of a rocket ride.

On July 29, 1960, NASA performed its first test of an astronaut-ready Mercury capsule mounted atop an Atlas rocket. The launch looked good until after the rocket disappeared from sight into the stormy upper atmosphere when it suddenly blew up, for no apparent reason. Gilruth decided the skin was too thin and needed strengthening. While adjustments were being made, NASA continued its test program using some of von Braun's Redstone rockets.

The first test of the Mercury-Redstone ran into the usual glitches. In early October 1960, just twenty-two minutes before the scheduled launch, a malfunction of the control system caused a postponement. Bad weather then forced NASA to scrub its November 7 makeup date. The delays in the program caused anxiety throughout the NASA staff. They counted heavily on a successful launch on November 21 to quiet critics of the U.S. program.

This time the launch went forward as scheduled. Clouds of smoke and brilliant flames roared from the bottom of the MR-1 as it jumped upward. A television camera panned up into the air, trying to track its progress, and lost sight of it. After an awkward pause, the camera panned back down to the launchpad to find the rocket had settled back after a four-inch flight. Adding to the comedy of the scene, parachutes deployed, and smoke and dye bombs designed to mark its location for recovery teams went off on the stationary craft.

NASA critics had a field day. The manned spaceflight plans had to be set back further while the flaws were ironed out. It was not until February 1961 that NASA was finally able to successfully launch a Mercury-Atlas rocket.

Meanwhile, on January 31, 1961, NASA tried one last animal trial in a test of its rockets' carrying capacity. A 37-pound chimpanzee named Ham was launched in a 2,400-pound capsule aboard a Redstone rocket to a height of 155 miles. Like Miss Sam, Ham was trained to perform simple in-flight tasks, such as watching for lights and flipping a toggle to get tasty banana pellets. The flight, however, brought more cause for concern. The rocket rose at too steep an angle, used up its liquid oxygen too soon, and overshot its target. Furthermore, holes had developed in the bottom of the capsule and it had begun to sink by the time the navy rescued it and the chimp.

DOGS IN SPACE

While the United States had trouble even getting off the ground, the Soviets' Vostok

A chimpanzee named Ham was sent into space to test the carrying capacity of NASA's rockets. Problems arose during the flight, bringing more cause for concern.

program ran into a few problems of its own. A dramatic attempt to send a rocket to Mars went nowhere. The first launching of an unmanned Vostok on May 15, 1960, designed to test the capsule and its retro-rocket system of maneuvering, was a mixed success. The capsule performed fine, but the rockets misfired, sending the capsule into higher orbit (where it stayed until 1965) rather than bringing it down as planned.

Korolev quickly made the needed corrections and in July made a more dramatic attempt at spaceflight. This time two dogs were placed in the capsule. The R-7 rocket that powered the flight, however, exploded upon ignition. The Vostok and the dogs were instantly destroyed. As usual, the disaster was hidden from the rest of the world.

Undaunted, Korolev returned to the launchpad less than a month later with another R-7, Vostok, and two more dogs. This time the launch went off perfectly, and the two dogs, Belka and Strelka, spent a day in space orbiting the earth. The Soviets then undertook the crucial task of getting the dogs back to earth safely. The revised retro-rocket positioning systems, heat shield, and parachutes worked well. The Vostok landed safely with the dogs in good health. The flight ended all doubt about humans riding in space; the Soviets had shown that it was possible to bring a living creature back safely through the terrors of reentry.

Flushed with success, the Soviets decided to put a man in space by the end of the year. But two subsequent failures, including one in December in which two dogs burned up in reentry, forced postponement of the plan. Only after two successful flights, both with dogs, in March 1961, were the Soviets willing to risk the life of a cosmonaut in space.

TO RACE OR NOT TO RACE

Throughout 1960 NASA directors worked hard on plans to beat the Russians in space accomplishments. Von Braun set to work developing a new supercharged Saturn rocket capable of lifting many tons of equipment into space. Other NASA scientists drew up programs that would build on the knowledge gained during the Mercury flights and test the technol-ogy and techniques required for further exploration, such as landing a man on the moon.

Eisenhower was appalled by the cost of these programs—estimated at up to $46 billion. His Scientific Advisory Committee agreed that they were both risky and a waste of money. "It will be the most expensive funeral a man has ever had,"[33] scoffed George Kistiakowsky, one of Eisenhower's expert advisers, about a possible manned moon shot. The Eisenhower administration decided to cut off all funding for manned spaceflights once the modest earth-orbiting Mercury program was complete.

During the 1960 presidential campaign, John Kennedy made an issue of Soviet dominance in space and what he called the lack of American leadership that allowed it to happen. Yet after winning the election and taking office in January 1961, Kennedy showed no more enthusiasm than Eisenhower for the massive spending required for NASA projects. His top science adviser, Jerome Weisner, argued that the United States should reconsider its plans to put a human in space. He was convinced that unmanned scientific probes would gather far more valuable information at a fraction of the cost of manned flights. "We should stop advertising Mercury as our major objective in space activities," said Weisner. "Indeed, we should make an effort to diminish the significance of this program."[34]

NASA director James Webb pleaded with the new administration to provide funds for the Gemini program, which was to follow up on the achievements of Mercury. If it failed to do so, said Webb, "it guarantees that the Russians will, for the next five to ten years, beat us to every spectacular exploratory flight."[35]

Although highly competitive, Kennedy had many of the same doubts as Eisenhower about committing so many of the nation's resources to a space race. He groped for some less extravagant way that the United States could demonstrate its technological prowess. But nothing he could think of could blunt the Soviet propaganda windfall that their space program was reaping.

In April 1961 Kennedy turned to his vice president, Lyndon Johnson, for advice. Johnson, whom Kennedy had assigned to chair the National Space Council, was one of the most powerful allies the space program had. It was Johnson who encouraged Kennedy to support von Braun's super-rocket program.

A strong ally of the space program, Vice President Lyndon Johnson encouraged President Kennedy to support von Braun's super-rocket project.

Kennedy asked Johnson what project the United States could undertake that had a good chance of beating the Russians. Johnson suggested landing a person on the moon. He cited NASA analysis showing that although the Soviets had more powerful rockets and were further ahead in space technology, they had done no better than the United States in developing a strategy and technology for landing a person on the moon. Still Kennedy hedged. His science experts told him that there was no way to guarantee beating the Soviets even if he approved the most expensive crash program possible.

On April 6 scientific research expert Vannevar Bush tried to dissuade Kennedy from a major space commitment. "Soviet space achievements have merely hurt our pride," said Bush. "The days when men will be in space for long periods and for varied purposes are so far off we need not hurry."[36] Any way Kennedy looked at it, the benefits of a space race seemed awfully small compared to the cost.

GAGARIN'S HISTORIC RIDE

While Kennedy was debating what to do, NASA geared up to put an end to the Soviets' string of space triumphs. Although the Atlas rocket still needed some fine-tuning, von Braun's Redstone rockets had shown they were powerful enough to launch a small Mercury capsule. The United States scheduled its historic launching of an astronaut into space for April 25, 1961. Navy lieutenant commander Alan Shepard was chosen for the

honor of riding the rocket over a hundred miles into the air, higher than any person had ever flown before.

While NASA finalized its plans, a twenty-seven-year-old air force pilot, so small that he had to sit on a pillow to fly a plane, stood at the base of an R-7 rocket at the Soviets' Baikonur Cosmodrome on a remote plain in Kazakhstan, a state in the south-central part of the Soviet Union. Dressed in a bulky orange suit, Yuri Gagarin addressed a small crowd of dignitaries with the simple words, "Senior Lieutenant Gagarin is ready for the first flight in the spaceship Vostok."[37]

With that, he ascended into the five-ton sphere atop the rocket. At 9:06 A.M. on April 12, the rocket ignited, sending Gagarin careening into space. Unlike the U.S. planned spaceflight, which was simply an up-and-down ride of a few minutes, the Soviets put Gagarin into orbit 187 miles above the earth. After a single orbit that lasted about ninety minutes, the Soviets prepared to bring their cosmonaut home.

The *Vostok 1* fired its retro-rockets on time and put the space capsule in the correct reentry position. But when the rockets shut down, Gagarin felt a sharp jolt. Looking out his window, he saw his spacecraft spinning out of control. For ten terrifying minutes the *Vostok 1* continued to tumble. Gagarin's life was saved when the retro-rockets finally broke loose and the spinning stopped. At twenty-three thousand feet, the hatch of his spacecraft blew open, firing Gagarin and his ejection seat into the air. He drifted down in his parachute and landed safely in a field

Cosmonaut Yuri Gagarin became the first man in space on April 12, 1961. The flight nearly ended in disaster when his spacecraft spun out of control during reentry.

near the Volga River, to the astonishment of the farmers working there.

Kennedy's Challenge

Soviet premier Nikita Khrushchev proclaimed Gagarin the Columbus of the twentieth century. Milking the triumph for all it was worth, he boasted about the superiority of the Soviet communist system and ridiculed the failures of the Americans. Kennedy fumed. He began to see space exploration not as a scientific endeavor but as a fundamental piece of strategy in the Cold War.

Kennedy was not the only one upset. Alan Shepard had been anticipating the honor of being the first person in space. A series of delays—many of them caused by NASA doctors and their extreme caution in allowing a man in space—had robbed him and his country of that glory. Publicly, Shepard held his frustration in check and awaited his upstaged moment in space.

That moment was subject to usual delays that continually plagued the U.S. space program. His flight, originally scheduled for May 2, was postponed until May 5 because of technical problems. Shepard awoke at 1:05 A.M. that day for the arduous preparations for space, which included

HOW WE DID IT, NOT WHEN

Alan Shepard was deeply frustrated by the Mercury project delays that enabled Gagarin to beat him into space. But at a May 1967 banquet, cited by James Schefter in The Race: The Uncensored Story of How America Beat Russia to the Moon, *he graciously offered an endorsement of NASA's space philosophy.*

"We were so close to the event that the country needed.

I pointed out a different decision could have given us the first flight—and could just as easily have ended in failure. I supported that decision then and I still support it today. . . .

I want every chance for this country to be first in everything it does. And yet, if we should lose the race to the moon, say for example, by a month, we cannot be more than temporarily dismayed. The important thing is that our decision is to pay for and project the technology that this country must have to maintain this leadership and to prove, and to improve, our domestic standards. My point is that we will be remembered in fact for how we did it, and not when we did it. And that our decisions next week and next year were made with the same courage and convictions displayed in 1961."

Frustrated by delays in the Mercury project, astronaut Alan Shepard nevertheless fully supported NASA's approach to putting an American in space.

having medical instruments attached to his body and donning a thirty-two-pound space suit. At 9:34, before a television audience of millions, he flew into the air in his ten-foot-long, 2,800-pound, bell-shaped *Freedom 7*, powered by a Redstone rocket.

The flight was a weak anticlimax to the Soviets' feat. Shepard did not orbit the earth. His spaceship achieved only one-fourth the speed that Gagarin's craft had managed three weeks earlier and covered only a fraction of the distance. He did, however, manage one thing that Gagarin did not. While Gagarin merely rode the capsule through space, Shepard briefly maneuvered his ship by firing small rockets.

Despite the modest accomplishments of *Freedom 7* compared to the Russians, the fact that the United States was able to launch a man 115 miles into the air aboard

KENNEDY'S CHALLENGE

Kennedy's ringing challenge to the nation and to the Soviets stands as one of the most memorable speeches of his short presidency. John M. Logsden, author of The Decision to Go to the Moon, *is among many who have quoted part of this speech:*

"I believe that this nation should commit itself to achieving the goal, before this decade is out, of landing a man on the moon and returning him safely to earth. No single space project in this period will be more impressive to mankind, or more important for the long-range exploration of space; and none will be so difficult or expensive to accomplish.

In a very real sense, it will not be one man going to the moon—we make this judgment affirmatively—it will be an entire nation. For all of us must work to put him there. . . .

I am asking the Congress and the country to accept a firm commitment to a new course of action. . . . If we are to go only halfway, or reduce our sights in the face of difficulty, in my judgment it would be better not to go at all . . . .

No one can predict with certainty what the ultimate meaning will be of the mastery of space. I believe we should go to the moon. But I think every citizen of this country . . . should consider the matter carefully . . . and there is no sense in agreeing or desiring that the United States take an affirmative position in outer space unless we are prepared to do the work and bear the burdens to make it successful."

Before Congress on May 25, 1961, President Kennedy challenged the nation to land a man on the moon and return him to the earth before the end of the decade.

a rocket and get him home again was a moral victory for NASA. At least they had proved they were still in the game.

Following Gagarin's ride, Kennedy consulted Bob Gilruth about the differences between the space programs of the superpowers. Gilruth insisted that the Soviet flights were largely public relations gimmicks. Their main advantage was in having a bigger rocket, but even the Soviets' R-7 had nowhere near the power needed to get a man to the moon. Gilruth insisted that with proper funding, NASA could overtake the Soviets and win the race to the moon.

On May 25, 1961, Kennedy finally accepted the Soviet space challenge. In an address to Congress, he challenged them to authorize $40 billion to the NASA program. "I believe that this nation should commit itself to achieving the goal, before this decade is out, of landing a man on the moon and re-

turning him safely to earth,"[38] said Kennedy.

The president still would not have minded an escape from the costly challenge the Soviets had coaxed out of him. Two weeks after making that address, he proposed to Khrushchev that the two countries pool their resources in a cooperative effort to reach the moon. Khrushchev declined, oddly enough, not because of Soviet superiority but rather its weakness. The Soviet premier was afraid that cooperation with the Americans would reveal how few nuclear missiles the country actually had, a situation that he feared could provoke an American attack.

The race was on. From this point, there was no turning back. Having publicly declared the space race to be a challenge to the character of the nation, Kennedy committed the nation to a winner-take-all competition with the Soviets to land an astronaut on the moon.

Chapter

5 Reaching Toward the Moon

Before they could even think about beating the Soviets to the moon, the United States had some catching up to do. On July 21, 1961, astronaut Gus Grissom extended Shepard's success by soaring 118 miles into the air before landing in the Atlantic Ocean. The mission nearly ended in disaster, however, when a device for opening the hatch triggered prematurely. Water poured into Grissom's *Liberty Bell 7*, causing it to sink. Grissom had to bail out of the foundering capsule and despite water that leaked into his suit through an open hose vent, dragging him underwater, managed to stay afloat long enough to be rescued.

Two weeks later the Soviets put on a show that made Grissom's small advance seem insignificant. Whereas Grissom's journey in space lasted only sixteen minutes, Gherman Titov in *Vostok 2*, spent an entire day in his orbiting capsule. After seventeen trips around the earth, during which the cosmonaut took time to sleep, he returned to earth safely. Premier Khrushchev wasted no time before gloating on his nation's latest victory in their declared race. "Titov's feat has shown once again what Soviet man, educated by the Communist Party, is able to do,"[39] boasted Khrushchev.

This put enormous pressure on NASA to step up its pace, but Gilruth refused to cut any corners just for appearances' sake. He insisted that the United States needed one last test flight before risking the life of an astronaut on a spaceflight around the world. That meant one last animal trial. On November 29, 1961, the United States launched a chimpanzee named Enos into orbit. After Enos flew two laps around the earth, NASA retrieved him and his capsule successfully.

GLENN AND THE HEAT SHIELD SCARE

On February 20, 1962, following a few days of the usual technical delays, marine pilot John Glenn blasted into the sky before fifty thousand spectators lining the Florida beaches and an estimated 100 million television viewers worldwide. Glenn reached orbiting height and made three circuits of the earth, monitored the entire way by the series of tracking stations.

The nation's euphoria over having finally put a man in orbit was tempered by tension in the NASA control room. During the second orbit, the capsule gave off a signal indicating that the heat shield had deployed. If the heat shield, in fact, had come loose, Glenn was a dead man—he and his unprotected capsule would burn up upon reentry. While hoping it was merely a faulty signal, NASA controllers had to assume the signal was correct. They decided to leave the retro-rocket pack on during reentry and hope that straps holding it in place would keep the shield on long enough to do its job. Doing so, however, could damage the heat shield badly enough that it would not work. Worse yet, if there was any fuel left in the

After entering his space capsule (below), John Glenn blasted off (right) before fifty-thousand local spectators and 100 million television viewers.

John Glenn prepares to reenter the earth's atmosphere. A faulty signal indicated that the capsule's heat shield was loose, making the reentry even more dangerous.

retropack, the capsule would explode in flames.

Glenn survived the reentry, although the retention of the retropack caused it to be far rougher than usual. As it turned out, Glenn took that risk for nothing—the indicator showing the deployment of the heat shield turned out to be in error. But the difficulties were forgotten in the national celebration that followed Glenn's mission. The United States had, at last, put a human into orbit.

GETTING IT RIGHT

A few weeks after Glenn's mission, Scott Carpenter ran into problems of a different nature on his three-orbit mission. In testing the thrusters that were designed to help maneuver the craft, Carpenter used up too much fuel. Then heating problems forced him to get behind in his checklist before reentry. In his rush, Carpenter missed a few items. The space capsule fell out of alignment, and Carpenter had barely enough fuel left to correct it before reentry. With flaming pieces of his heat shield flying off, he overshot the landing area so badly that recovery teams couldn't reach him until nearly forty-five minutes after landing.

With relentless thoroughness, the NASA teams corrected all problems they encountered. The final flights of astronauts Wally Schirra and Gordon Cooper went so smoothly that Gilruth decided they could skip the final scheduled Mercury flight and go right on to the next program—Gemini.

PROJECT GEMINI

NASA officials knew that neither the Soviet Union nor the United States could get to the moon with the present technology. Both sides would have to gather new information on the capabilities of humans in space. They needed to determine the physical and mental effects of prolonged periods of weightlessness and close confinement under stress. They needed to develop precision in their

The Gemini capsule, shown under construction, was designed to carry two astronauts.

launches so that crucial timetables could be followed. They had to discover the nature of the moon's surface—was it, as some astronomers speculated, a deep pile of dust, a thin crust that would crumble under pressure, or a rock-solid landing surface?

Researchers would have to design and build new equipment, components, and materials. They needed to invent giant rockets that could carry many tons of equipment to the moon, a lightweight vehicle that could both land on the moon and launch a successful return flight, and instruments of maneuverability so advanced that spacecraft could rendezvous and dock in outer space and astronauts could move around outside the spacecraft. All equipment, materials, and systems had to be rigorously tested to ensure that the mission to the moon could be accomplished safely. In late 1961 NASA initiated Project Gemini as a program to accomplish this testing. The Gemini name referred to mythological twins and highlighted the fact that each launch in the program would carry two astronauts.

HOW TO GET THERE

The most important decision NASA faced in the moon race was the basic strategy for getting to the moon and back. According to NASA official Owen Maynard, "We had more harebrained schemes than you could shake a stick at."[40] Three courses of action eventually came to the fore in the planning for Project Apollo, which started even before Project Gemini got under way. The simplest method was direct ascent to the moon. Launching a spaceship that could land on the moon and then return to earth would require few steps, a minimum of parts, little coordination, and no intricate rendezvous techniques. This method gained the support of many, including von Braun, Kennedy adviser Jerome Weisner, and William Pickering of JPL. Its main drawback was that it would require an incredibly powerful rocket to haul a spaceship, astronauts, and all equipment required for both the round-trip journey and any moon exploration. Even the most optimistic estimates conceded that such a ship would weigh at least seventy-five tons, roughly forty times that of a Mercury capsule. Rocket experts were not even sure such a rocket could be launched from land because of the tremendous noise and vibration it would create.

The second choice was to scale back the rocket requirements by using an earth orbital rendezvous. In this scenario, two rockets would be launched close together. One would contain the space capsule, the other would carry extra fuel. After reaching orbit, the capsule would rendezvous with the supply ship to take on the fuel it needed. This proposal never gained much support and was abandoned fairly early in the debate.

The third method, the lunar orbit rendezvous, involved far more coordination than the other two. As far back as the early 1950s, *Time* magazine had suggested that the most practical means of moon exploration was for a spaceship to orbit the moon and send "small space-dinghies down to explore the surface."[41] In the early 1960s, NASA's John Houbolt argued for a similar plan. He proposed launching a command module (CM) containing three astronauts toward the moon. The CM would be attached to a second spacecraft called the lunar excursion module (eventually shortened to LM). While one astronaut piloted the CM in orbit around the moon, the LM would carry the other two to the moon's surface. When their mission on the moon was finished, they would return to the command module and head back to earth.

The disadvantage of the system was that it required more technology, equipment, and coordination than the other approaches. But by eliminating many tons from the return launch, it would be far more practical and inexpensive. Not only could the LM be smaller and more lightweight than a direct ascent spacecraft, it would not need the heat shield required for reentry (the CM would provide that), nor the tons of fuel necessary for liftoff.

For two years Houbolt fought heavy opposition in arguing for the lunar orbit approach. Gradually, though, many of his colleagues came to agree with him. According to Maynard, "I guess that a minute after the meeting we probably thought it wasn't a very good idea." But they kept coming back to it and found that "when you take all of the different ways of doing things into consideration, when you've got a chance to digest them, and ask a few thousand more questions, it begins to make more sense."[42] In April 1962 NASA director Webb and Kennedy approved the lunar orbiting method.

PUSHING THE LUNAR-ORBIT RENDZEVOUS

While there is considerable debate over where the idea for the lunar orbital rendezvous originated, NASA engineer John Houbolt is credited as the strongest advocate of the method during the debate with champions of other methods. In T. A. Heppenheimer's Countdown: A History of Space Flight, *Houbolt describes how he came to be involved in the fight.*

"I can still remember the 'back of the envelope' type of calculations I made to check that the scheme resulted in a very substantial saving in earth boost requirements. Almost spontaneously it became clear that lunar-orbit rendezvous offered a chain-reaction simplification on all back effects: development, testing, manufacturing, erection, countdown, flight operations, etc. All would be simplified. The thought struck my mind, 'This is fantastic. If there is any idea we have to push, it is this one!' I vowed to dedicate myself to the task."

SPACE EXPLORATION ON HOLD

Because so much of the technology required for a moon shot was nonexistent, NASA's launchpad went dormant for a couple of years while its top people laid the groundwork for the program. Albert Thomas, who had represented Houston in Congress since 1937, used his considerable influence to get NASA a gigantic new Manned Spacecraft Center in Houston. NASA recruited and trained nine more astronauts. Engineers spent the time designing a larger capsule with a skin made of a stronger, lighter-weight metal alloy. Despite this, the capsule still had too much weight for the Atlas used in Mercury launches, and so the rocket experts put together a new Titan missile. Scientists and engineers spent long hours working on the problem of pro-

viding water and power for a long-term flight without carrying along a great deal of weight. Their innovative solution was the fuel cell. By mixing liquid oxygen and hydrogen, the fuel cell could create a chemical reaction that provided these necessities.

MORE SOVIET FIRSTS

The start-up time required for the Gemini program gave the Soviets a clear path to another series of stunning firsts in the moon race. After a year-long absence in space while they manufactured new, more maneuverable Vostoks, the Soviets sprang back into action in the summer of 1962. On August 11 Andrian Nikolayev blasted into space in *Vostok 3*, followed only a day later by Pavel Popovich in *Vostok 4*.

The ability to carry off two launches within such a short span was a major achievement. But Korolev's real purpose in the mission was to achieve a space rendezvous between the two capsules. Popovich's trajectory carried him into a slightly higher orbit. That meant that his orbits were slightly longer than Nikolayev's. Over the next day, Nikolayev's *Vostok 3* gradually closed the distance until it drew within sight of *Vostok 4*, a distance of 3.2 miles.

Each spacecraft logged over a million miles, and Nikolayev set a new record by staying in orbit for four days, covering sixty-four circuits of the earth. He and Popovich then landed safely within six minutes of each other, about 150 miles apart.

Many international observers were impressed by the Soviets' display of precise coordination. Sir Bernard Lovell of England's Jodrell Bank Observatory was moved to say, "I think the Russians are so far ahead in the technique of rocketry that the possibility of America catching up in the next decade is remote."[43]

NASA scientists, however, considered the mission more show than substance. They noted that the cosmonauts had no means of controlling their modules; after closing to 3.2 miles, they steadily drifted apart. Their closing to 3.2 miles had been a simple matter of trajectories. No amount of calculation could coordinate two spacecraft's flights so precisely as to allow them to dock, which appeared to be a necessity for a moon shot. In terms of the space race, therefore, the Soviets' feat was meaningless.

Early the next summer, Korolev had another surprise in store for his rivals. On June 14, 1963, he sent Valery Bykovsky up in *Vostok 5*. While orbiting for a record five days, Bykovsky slipped off the restraining straps in his compartment and floated in zero gravity for ninety minutes. This demonstration of how easily humans could adapt to weightless conditions was followed by a public relations bonanza. While Bykovsky was in orbit, Korolev launched *Vostok 6*, carrying Valentina Tereshkova. At a time when the United States was not even considering women for the role, this first woman in space completed forty-nine orbits during her three days in space. As in the previous Soviet rendezvous effort, her craft passed within about three miles of *Vostok 5*, at which time she established radio contact with Bykovsky. The flight appeared to prove that Soviet space technology was so advanced that even a nonpilot could operate their space vehicles. But again U.S. experts noted that the Soviets had not built in any pilot maneuvering mechanism. The cosmonauts remained passengers and not pilots.

SECOND THOUGHTS

In the fall of 1963, Kennedy repeated his offer to Khrushchev to join forces in their lunar program. By this time the United States had a clear idea of Soviet missile strength, and so Khrushchev had nothing to hide. But while he was considering the plan, Kennedy was assassinated. A year later militants forced Khrushchev out of office, and the idea of space cooperation was shelved for the duration of the moon race.

Cosmonaut Valentina Tereshkova became the first female to fly in space. At the time, the United States was not even considering sending a woman into orbit.

Despite the Soviets' space superiority, Khrushchev may have been tempted by the offer because the Soviet space program had centered on short-term successes at the expense of a long-term program. It was not until 1964 that the Communist Party of the Soviet Union approved a lunar landing as a national objective, and even then it was not given high priority.

Meanwhile, in the nearly two years between the Mercury and Gemini flights, the United States began to lose its enthusiasm for the space race. Kennedy was dead, and although his successor, Lyndon Johnson, supported NASA, it was not with the same competitive fury that motivated Kennedy. As the Soviets' continuing victory streak in space technology took its toll on U.S. morale, the United States began cutting NASA's budget.

SPACE WALK

Gemini brought the United States back to the launchpad in April 1964 with a successful unmanned test of the new space module and rocket. But before the

Americans could resume sending astronauts in space, Korolev struck again. Noting that the Gemini program was designed for two astronauts, he wanted to up the ante by launching a spaceship with three cosmonauts. However, the space vehicles designed to accommodate this number, the Soyuz series, were not scheduled to be ready until 1967. According to NASA's timetable, which was public knowledge, the United States would be finished with its Gemini program by then and into its own three-man Apollo program.

Determined to stay ahead of the Americans, Korolev had one of his chief designers, Konstantin Feoktistov, redesign the one-man Vostok capsule into a three-man Voskhod. He eliminated the ejection seats in favor of retro-rockets and a second parachute that would bring the spacecraft down safely. The bulky space suits had to be scrapped, which meant the compartment had to contain a livable atmosphere and be absolutely airtight. The first Voskhod test model was launched on October 6, 1964. After completing one orbit, the unmanned unit landed safely.

Six days later Feoktistov went up in the spacecraft he designed, crammed into the compartment along with pilot Vladimir Komarov and Boris Yegorov, a doctor. The three spent a day in orbit before landing safely, giving the Soviets the first multi-person spaceflight.

Shortly thereafter Korolev's knowledge of the U.S. space timetable again allowed him to one-up the Americans. Aware that NASA was planning a space walk in the near future, Korolev rushed to carry out an identical mission. However, the first of two specially built Voskhods exploded during an unmanned test in February 1965. With no time to build or test another space vehicle, Korolev could beat the United States only by taking a huge risk. On March 18 he sent Pavel Belyayev and Aleksei Leonov up in the remaining, unproven Voskhod.

Soon after reaching orbit, Leonov, wearing a specially designed suit, crawled into an air-lock passage. He clipped a lifeline to the Voskhod, activated a switch that opened the outer door, and drifted out into space. "I . . . stretched out my arms and legs and soared,"[44] reported Leonov. For ten minutes he walked in the vast unknown, snapping photographs.

The Soviets' latest triumph nearly ended in disaster, twice. Leonov's suit swelled up so much under the pressurized oxygen he was breathing that he could not get back in the door. Only after several attempts at bleeding enough oxygen from the suit was he able to make it. Then, in reentry, the retro-rocket system failed. Belyayev had to maneuver the capsule using one of the two rockets that was designed to cushion the landing. They veered twelve hundred miles off course and landed in the trees of a forest so dense that the Soviets could not air-drop a rescue crew. The cosmonauts spent a miserable freezing night in the trees before escaping the next morning and welcoming a rescue team.

GEMINI GETS OFF THE GROUND

The Gemini program had four primary objectives in paving the way for the

AMERICA'S NEW SUPERSTARS

In January of 1959 NASA began requesting recommendations from military commanders for test pilots to fill the newly created positions of astronauts. These pilots had to be between the ages of twenty-five and forty and, because of capsule size and rocket power limitations, could be no larger than five feet eleven inches and 180 pounds.

From an initial list of 508 candidates, NASA summoned 108 to Washington, D.C., without telling them anything about the program. The list was eventually pared down to 32 who agreed to undergo a grueling battery of tests. These included psychological exams, sensory deprivation, endurance tests, such as how long they could keep their feet in ice water, and humiliating invasions of privacy as doctors probed every aspect of their health. From this data, in April 1959 NASA chose seven astronauts: air force pilots Gus Grissom, Deke Slayton, and Gordon Cooper; navy pilots Wally Schirra, Scott Carpenter, and Alan Shepard; and marine pilot John Glenn.

NASA failed to anticipate the overwhelming media interest in the nation's new space pioneers. The huge media blitz that greeted the press conference at which their appointments were announced, plus a series of stories by *Life* magazine, which paid them all a total of $500,000 per year for their personal stories, made them instant celebrities.

The first seven astronauts selected by NASA became instant celebrities.

A Soviet postcard recreates Leonov's space walk. Leonov soared in orbit for ten minutes.

moon landing: determine whether astronauts could safely and effectively operate in a space capsule for the two weeks that a mission to the moon would require; perfect the techniques of rendezvous and docking required for a lunar orbital landing; gain expertise in spacewalking, which might be needed to make repairs and adjustments outside the capsule; and develop expertise in launching and landing in a timely and efficient way.

On March 23, 1965, the United States broke its period of dormancy in manned spaceflight by launching *Gemini 3*, with Gus Grissom and John Young at the controls. The goals for the three-orbit flight were modest. First, NASA wanted to test the functionality and comfort of the cabin. On this score, *Gemini 3* barely passed; Young likened the accommodations to "sitting in a phone booth that was lying on its side."[45] Second, NASA needed to see if the larger built-in thruster rockets provided the maneuverability that future space rendezvous would require. The results of this test were encouraging. The astronauts found they could slow their spacecraft by turning it completely around and firing the rockets against their momentum. By turning the capsule ninety degrees and firing rockets, they could move sideways or up and down. The flight greatly encouraged NASA officials, for despite the Soviets' far grander accomplishments, their Voskhods could not begin to match the maneuverability of the Gemini.

Three months later NASA took direct aim at some of the Soviets' proud accomplishments. On June 3, 1965, it launched *Gemini 4*, the first spaceship to be equipped with an onboard computer—one of the successes of the U.S. focus on miniaturization. Astronauts Ed White and James McDivitt stayed aloft for ninety-eight hours, during which they lapped the earth sixty-three times. For the first time in the space race, the United States claimed the record for the longest spaceflight.

White then leapfrogged past the Soviet's heralded space walk. NASA officials, after studying a video of Leonov moving clumsily on his space walk, devised a "zip gun" that allowed an astronaut to control his movements through bursts of pressurized oxygen. The gun worked beautifully. White so enjoyed his frolic outside the spacecraft that his scheduled twelve-minute exercise stretched to twenty before NASA officials in Houston ordered him back into *Gemini 4*. Getting back into the spacecraft proved no problem, although White had some trouble getting the bulky hatch closed.

McDivitt had less success in his attempt to rendezvous with a Titan second-stage rocket that was floating in orbit from a previous launch. Piloting a spacecraft, he discovered to his frustration, was not the same as piloting an airplane. Every time he fired a rocket thruster in an attempt to get closer, the burst moved his spaceship into higher orbit and he ended up farther away. After using up most of his fuel in a futile attempt to get closer, the effort was abandoned.

That was but a minor setback, however. The rest of the *Gemini 4* flight was such a success that President Johnson proclaimed that the United States had caught up with the Soviets in the space race. Most experts were not yet ready to go that far, but for the first time it appeared as though the United States had a chance of overtaking the Russians' efforts.

RENDEZVOUS

For the next year and a half, NASA sent up a steady stream of Gemini spacecraft, one every two months. In August 1965 Gordon Cooper and Pete Conrad flew *Gemini 5* in what was primarily a longevity test. The astronauts had little to do other than testing the recently developed fuel cells, which had a few glitches, and the new rendezvous radar, which worked fine. Although they described the ordeal as spending "eight days in a garbage can,"[46] they completed the flight with little difficulty.

NASA officials looked forward to *Gemini 6* with special anticipation. On this flight Wally Schirra and Tom Stafford would attempt a maneuver that was far more sophisticated than anything the Soviets had tried. They were to use their radar to home in on an Agena target vehicle that would be sent up just prior to their launch. Unfortunately, the Agena blew up before the astronauts left the pad.

Rather than try to repeat the experiment, NASA made the bold move of skipping that test and moving on to a rendezvous between two Gemini capsules. On December 4, 1965, Frank Borman and James Lovell rode *Gemini 7* into orbit and waited for Stafford and Schirra to arrive in *Gemini 6*.

Eight days later *Gemini 6* sat on the launchpad. The rocket flamed with a thunderous roar and then went silent. NASA officials blanched, fearing the rocket might explode. According to safety procedures, Schirra and Stafford should have ejected. Had they done so, the mission would have been canceled. But they did not, no explosion occurred, and technicians soon found the loose components that caused the malfunction. On December 15 the tardy *Gemini 6* finally soared into orbit.

Initially, it lagged fourteen hundred miles behind *Gemini 7*, which flew in a higher orbit. By firing orbital thrusters, Schirra gained speed and raised his orbit. He then maneuvered his craft sideways to get on the same orbital path as his target. Eventually, his radar locked onto the target, and the astronauts saw what appeared to be a bright star. Schirra fired his rockets again to close the gap. A little more than a mile away from *Gemini 7*, he began braking by firing forward thrusters. The control problems that McDivitt had experienced had been solved, and *Gemini 6* coasted to within thirty feet of the target.

The two ships returned, *Gemini 7* having stayed in orbit for two full weeks. The experience left Borman and Lovell shaky, suffering from dizzy spells, weakened muscles, and blood pooling in their lower legs. But they shrugged these off as minor nuisances and confirmed that humans could handle the long flight to the moon.

DOCKING

Gemini 8's mission was to not only rendezvous but to actually dock with an Agena target vehicle and join the two to form a single spacecraft. On March 18, 1966, two days after takeoff, Neil Armstrong and Dave Scott caught up with the target and braked to within fifty yards. From there they achieved such control with their thrusters that they moved in at the rate of three inches per second. Before long they achieved the remarkable breakthrough of docking with another space vehicle.

They nearly did not live to tell about it. Thirty minutes after docking, the joined spacecraft began rolling. It got so bad that Armstrong, thinking the Agena was causing the problem, temporarily slowed the roll rate with his thrusters, undocked and backed away.

Instead the roll increased. "We have a serious problem here,"[47] reported Scott as the roll accelerated to a vision-blurring rate of nearly one revolution per second. Fighting to keep from passing out, Armstrong shut off the orbital altitude and maneuvering system, switched on his

The Gemini 7 *capsule is seen here from* Gemini 6. *The crews of the two spacecraft were able to maneuver their ships as close as thirty feet from each other.*

reentry control system, and fired jets that were able to stop the roll. It turned out that one of the thrusters had gotten stuck in the on position and fired continually, which nearly spun them into unconsciousness and would have made it impossible for them to pilot the spacecraft home. Having activated the reentry control system, the crew had no choice but to cut short their flight and perform an emergency landing on earth.

Gemini 9 ran into more problems in its docking attempt in May. First, the mission was postponed when the target Agena fell into the ocean. A backup Agena sailed into orbit, but when Gene Cernan and Tom Stafford caught up to it, they found they could not dock with it because the docking ring was snapping like an "angry alligator."[48] The problem was that a clamshell cover over the ring had failed to completely disengage. Cernan did, at least, manage a space walk, although even that exercise was marred by a clouded faceplate.

NASA engineers and technicians methodically ironed out every problem that arose. Gemini missions 10 through 12, all run in the latter half of 1966, performed nearly flawlessly. John Young and Michael Collins, in *Gemini 10*, docked with two Agena rockets. Collins used a zip gun to spacewalk over to the second target. Pete Conrad and Dick Gordon rode *Gemini 11* to 853 miles above the earth, nearly twice the previous record. Finally, James Lovell and Buzz Aldrin flew *Gemini 12*, in which Aldrin stayed outside the spacecraft for five and a half hours, testing his skill at working with tools in a zero-gravity environment.

Dave Scott (left) and Neil Armstrong pose with a model of a Gemini capsule docked with an Agena target vehicle. They almost didn't survive their mission.

THE GEMINI BARGAIN

Walter Cunningham, an astronaut who flew in the first Apollo mission, described the significance of the Gemini program in his book The All-American Boys:

"[Gemini] was the proving ground for nearly every critical step of the space program for the next ten years. Although we were still feeling our way, the Gemini spacecraft was not the experimental laboratory model of the Mercury program. It was produced on the nearest thing to an assembly line for space hardware we had seen so far, lifting off from Cape Kennedy at regular two-month intervals, and performing just fine. The program had been conceived as a gap filler between Mercury and Apollo, and it is now hard to imagine going to the moon without it. Gemini's contribution was purchased at the bargain-basement price of $1.5 billion."

The Gemini program was an astounding success. Every mission was carried out safely. Each experienced problems, all of which were eventually solved. In the flights, the Americans mastered precision maneuvers far beyond anything the Soviets had accomplished.

The question on everyone's mind was, what were the Soviets doing? During the entire Gemini program, they had not launched a single spaceflight. No one at NASA knew why, nor whether the United States had in fact jumped ahead in the space race.

6 The Grand Prize

Unknown to the Americans, the Soviet Union's challenge was in serious decline. By 1965 Korolev's focus on establishing space firsts at the expense of a long-range program had left serious gaps in his nation's space capability. The Soviets could not maneuver their spacecraft with anything close to the Americans' precision. Korolev's reliance on programmed technology had cut the cosmonaut out of all but the most elementary operational tasks. As the requirements of space exploration became more complex, it became increasingly difficult for the Soviets to predesign their equipment to handle every eventuality.

Furthermore, once the United States put its considerable financial and private industry resources behind the lunar project, it placed the less affluent Soviet society at a severe disadvantage. Recognizing that the odds were growing against him, Korolev began to pull back from all-out competition with the United States for a moon landing. Instead, he began to focus on a different space accomplishment—a space station.

But perhaps the most damaging blow to the Soviet moon race was the fate of its director. The respiratory problems that had plagued Korolev since his days as a prisoner in Siberia grew worse in the mid-1960s, sapping his energy. He then developed cancer and on January 14, 1966, underwent surgery to combat this disease. He died on the operating table of heart failure at the age of fifty-eight.

With Korolev gone, the Russian effort suffered through five months of infighting and confusion before Vasily Mishin assumed control. He inherited a mess. Lacking the genius and fanatical passion of Korolev, Mishin was unable to jump-start the stalled Soviet program. According to reporter James Schefter, "Most of the moon and planetary probes failed; their rockets blew up, their guidance systems missed the targets, or the hardware simply went dead out there in space and was never heard from again."[49]

NEW HARDWARE FOR APOLLO

Even with the success of Gemini, a number of potential pitfalls remained in the path of a U.S. moon shot. One of these was building a new rocket that could carry fifty tons of space vehicles to the moon. For his Saturn V rocket, von Braun used essentially the same design that had worked for him since the 1950s, only on an almost unimaginable scale. The first stage was the largest aluminum cylinder ever created—33 feet in diameter and 138 feet tall. It had held enough liquid oxygen and kerosene to fill fifty-four railroad cars, all of which would be totally consumed in three minutes of flight. The fuel pumps that fed propellant to the combustion chamber were larger than refrigerators, and the pipes that carried that fuel were big enough for a person to crawl through.

With the three other stages stacked on top of it, the Saturn V was the size of a Navy destroyer. It stood 363 feet tall, weighed nearly 6 million pounds, and was four times more powerful than any previous rocket. As mighty as it was, the Saturn V might not have been able to lift its incredible load were it not for a super-strong aluminum alloy developed jointly by the Alcoa and Reynolds companies.

The first stage of the Saturn V rocket was the largest aluminum cylinder ever built. At thirty-three feet in diameter and 138 feet tall, it held enough kerosene and liquid oxygen to fill fifty-four railroad cars.

This alloy made it possible for the rocket to be built with a lightweight skin only .64 centimeters (less than a quarter inch) thick.

A second key innovation for the Apollo moon-landing program was the lunar module. The LM looked more like a giant robot than a flying machine, with four bent landing legs protruding from the bottom, each with an aluminum shock absorber. Built by the Grumman Aircraft Engineering Corporation, it stood twelve feet high and weighed almost seventeen tons. The module contained no seats; the pilots would stand while flying in it.

The LM was an enormously complex piece of equipment that came about only because of recent advances in computer technology. As Joseph Gavin Jr., a vice president at Grumman, commented, "I'm sure you couldn't have designed this ve-hicle without a computer. None of us would have lived long enough."[50]

Computers allowed NASA engineers to simulate thousands of conditions that the astronauts might encounter in space. They tried to imagine every possible scenario so that any problems that arose could be identified and solved in advance of any actual crisis.

"WE'RE BURNING UP"

The Apollo program that was designed to put an American on the moon began with a series of unmanned test flights of various rocket and spacecraft components in late 1966. The first manned Apollo flight was scheduled for February 21, 1967.

About a month before that, the crew for that flight—Gus Grissom, Ed White, and

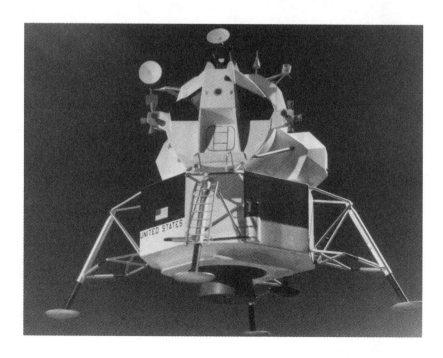

Seen here in the form of a model, the Apollo lunar module was an enormously complex piece of equipment that could not have been designed without advances in computer technology.

Roger Chaffee—donned their bulky space suits and entered a space capsule sitting on top of a Saturn 1-B rocket. It was a training exercise so routine that the backup crew flew off to Houston without even waiting for it to finish.

Suddenly a note of alarm sounded from the astronauts in the capsule. "We've got a bad fire—let's get out. . . . We're burning up."[51]

Tragically, the test was being run under flight conditions, which meant that the atmosphere of the cabin was hyperflammable pure oxygen. While the astronauts strained to escape the command module and rescue teams rushed to their aid, the fire roared into an inferno. An explosion ruptured the hull, throwing rescuers against a wall and inflicting burns. In a cruel irony, the capsule hatch had been redesigned so that it was bolted shut, as a response to the accidental opening of the hatch that had nearly drowned Grissom back in the Mercury program. That intended safety measure killed Grissom and his crewmates, all of whom died of asphyxiation. Ed White, the strongest of all the astronauts, could not pry the hatch open, and five and a half minutes passed before the rescue team could do the job.

The cause of the fire was never determined, although a spark or short circuit in the wiring was the most likely culprit. The tragedy nearly ended the Apollo program. All missions were put on hold, and NASA directors ordered every piece of equipment reexamined and tested for safety. They discovered that the cockpit was full of flammable objects such as couch covers, cushions, cooling system components, and even the space suits. An editorial in the *New York Times* on April 8, 1967, issued a devastating indictment after reading the investigative report on the fire: "The dry technical prose of the report convicts those in charge of Project Apollo of incompetence and negligence."[52]

It was the astronauts themselves who argued most strongly for continuing the space program. Grissom's own words, issued a month before his death, provided a rallying cry for NASA. "If we die, we want people to accept it," said Grissom. "We're in a risky business and we hope if anything happens to us, it will not delay the program."[53]

As it turned out, the tragedy of the *Apollo 1* crew was a wake-up call to NASA that may well have saved the moon project at a time when budget cuts were beginning to affect the space program. According to Chris Kraft, one of NASA's top administrators, their newly ordered review of all equipment found many problems with the spacecraft that could have delayed the program indefinitely. "We'd have flown, found problems, taken months to fix them, flown again, found more problems, taken more months. . . ."[54]

NASA engineers made 1,341 changes to the Apollo spacecraft in the two years following the fire. At one point astronaut Frank Borman lived at the North American Rockwell plant that was rebuilding the Apollo module. He was given the authority to approve, on the spot, any changes he deemed necessary.

Among the alterations was the removal of all flammable objects from the space

(Above) Astronauts Gus Grissom, Ed White, and Roger Chaffee were killed when their Apollo 1 capsule caught fire (right), but their deaths led to drastic improvements in equipment and safety procedures.

modules. As NASA scientist Tom Markely pointed out, this may have saved the program from a program-ending disaster. "If we had had the Apollo fire in orbit or going to the moon, we wouldn't have flown for decades."[55]

MORE TRAGEDY

Despite their problems in the mid-1960s, the Soviets had not given up the space competition. After conducting three unmanned spaceflights in March and April 1967, the Soviets were ready to try out their new Soyuz, a spacecraft that they believed could duplicate the U.S. rendezvous and docking procedures. On April 23, 1967, Vladimir Komarov went up into orbit alone in a roomy cockpit designed to hold three cosmonauts. U.S. analysts believed that his mission was to rendezvous and exchange crews with another Soyuz that was to follow him into orbit.

After nineteen circuits of the earth, however, Komarov began experiencing problems with the solar panels that provided his power source. Soviet officials had to cancel the rendezvous and bring him down early. The reentry proceeded flawlessly until one of the parachutes snarled upon opening. The Soyuz smashed into the ground, killing Komarov and ending the Soviets' hopes of capitalizing on the Americans' flight moratorium.

SATURN V TESTING

During the months of agonizing examination and redesign on the Apollo spacecraft, von Braun's rocket program provided a moment of reassurance. The sheer enormity of the Saturn V rocket required his team to spend two months checking it out after it was built. The force of its ignition was expected to be so great that its launchpad was constructed three and a half miles away from any building or personnel. Towing the giant rocket that distance took ten hours.

On November 9, 1967, von Braun's team fired up the rocket. As the liquid oxygen and fuel flooded into the combustion chambers of the five engines, the rocket roared to life with the force of a volcano. The Saturn lifted into the air without a problem and reached a top speed of twenty-five thousand miles per hour.

The United States now had a rocket powerful enough to send a spaceship and crew to the moon. In the words of Dale Myer, Apollo program manager for North American Rockwell, which built part of the rocket, "If you want to pick one really important element that caught us up to the Russians, it was the decision to go with the Saturn V booster. It gave us a big power capability in space, and that's really where you get your payoff."[56]

Meanwhile the lunar module passed its tests with flying colors. On January 22, 1968, NASA launched an unmanned, legless LM into orbit. Its engines were fired up by remote control and performed so well that NASA saw no need to go ahead with its next scheduled unmanned test.

The celebrations, however, turned to near despair in April 1968. On the final unmanned test launch, designated *Apollo 6*, the rocket lurched and chugged off the pad, shaking so viciously that von Braun was concerned a crew could be injured. Worse yet, two of the engines in stage two shut down, causing the rocket to fall short of its altitude goal. On top of that, the third stage failed to restart in orbit.

SOVIET MYSTERY

At this point most experts believed the United States was ahead in the space race, but doubts persisted. *Newsweek* magazine reflected a common feeling, noting, "There is the nagging suspicion that the Russians, formidable competitors in space for the last decade, might get to the moon first."[57]

The Soviet leadership claimed that they were not particularly interested in flying to the moon, but this struck many Americans as a defensive strategy. Said one U.S. diplomat, "They say they are not in the race so that in case they're beaten, they can say they never even tried."[58]

As it turned out, the Soviet space program did have some life left in it. Realizing that the odds of them landing a person on the moon before the United States were slim, they opted to be the first to fly to the moon. After several unsuccessful tests of its unmanned Zond spacecraft early in 1968, the Soviets finally succeeded in September in sending *Zond 5* to the moon. The spacecraft looped around the moon, closing to a distance of twelve hundred miles, and then returned to earth, its two passenger turtles arriving no worse for the wear.

NASA director James Webb admitted that this flight was "the most important demonstration of total space capacity up to now by any nation."[59] Some U.S. experts expected the Soviets to follow up on this by being the first to send a man around the moon, a mission the United States was still hoping to achieve by the end of the year.

CHRISTMAS MOON

Von Braun and his staff worked quickly to solve the problems with the Saturn V. They determined that the pogo effect during liftoff was caused by partial vacuums forming in the fuel line. This was corrected by adding pressurized helium to the system. The other problems were eliminated by strengthening the propellant lines to protect them from the rocket's tremendous heat.

The problems were corrected in time for Wally Schirra, Walt Cunningham, and Donn Eisele to try out the Apollo spacecraft. On October 11, 1968, they rode the *Apollo 7* into orbit and tested its systems for eleven days. Schirra gained a reputation as the good luck charm of NASA. As with his other two missions, this one went perfectly. That cleared the way for *Apollo 8* to go to the moon.

No Soviet manned flights to the moon were even on the drawing board in December when Frank Borman, Bill Anders, and James Lovell rode their *Apollo 8* spacecraft 240,000 miles through space toward the moon—that ancient object of human curiosity. The voyage was riskier than many observers realized, as a later flight would prove. On the *Apollo 13* mission, an oxygen tank exploded and the crew was able to survive only by using the lunar module as a refuge. Had that happened on *Apollo 8*, which did not carry a lunar module, the astronauts would have died.

On Christmas Eve, the crew used their thrusters to maneuver their craft into lunar orbit. An emotional crew read from the Bible as they became the first humans to get a closeup view of the moon. After ten orbits of the moon, during which they approached to within sixty miles, the astronauts returned home safely.

On March 3, 1969, *Apollo 9*, with Jim McDivitt, Dave Scott, and Rusty Schweickart aboard, roared into earth orbit. Their job was to test the LM's ability to detach from the command module in space, fire up its engine, and redock with the command module. Again, everything performed according to plan.

That left one final preparatory mission, which Tom Stafford, Gene Cernan, and John Young began on May 18. The mission of *Apollo 10* was to do everything but land on the moon. Upon reaching lunar

The earth is seen from lunar orbit during Apollo 8's *December, 1968, mission.*

orbit, Stafford and Cernan climbed into the LM and piloted it down to within forty-seven thousand feet of the moon's surface. Despite a moment of anxiety when their control system malfunctioned, sending their craft into wild gyrations, all systems worked fine.

The next mission was a moon landing; it looked as though NASA was going to beat Kennedy's deadline of landing a man on the moon before the end of the decade. The nagging suspicion lingered, though, that the Soviets would somehow spring a surprise as they had done so often in the past.

THE SOVIETS' SPRINT TO THE MOON

Much of the suspicion had to do with the Soviets' latest Soyuz rendezvous missions. Three days after *Apollo 7* landed in October

1968, Georgy Beregovoy rode alone in *Soyuz 3*. While in space he performed a rendezvous with a target rocket, coming within 650 feet of it before running out of fuel. Then, following *Apollo 8*, the Soviets performed a docking maneuver more complex than any the United States had tried. On January 14 Vladimir Shatalov blasted off in *Soyuz 4*. A day later Yevgeni Khrunov, Aleksei Yeliseyev, and Boris Volynov joined him in orbit in *Soyuz 5*. Shatalov caught his companions, and they were able to dock. Khrunov and Yeliseyev then walked out of *Soyuz 5* and moved into *Soyuz 4*. Both flights returned home safely a few days later. Meanwhile U.S. intelligence picked up reports of a mammoth new rocket, the N-1, designed to carry large loads.

Unknown to nervous American observers, Soyuz was not a moon shot program, but rather part of the Soviets' alternate mission to set up a permanent space station. As for the N-1, in early July 1969 it exploded on the launchpad during its first test flight with such force that it leveled the Baikonur launch facility, killing more than a hundred workers in the process. The devastation was so complete that it would take the Soviets two years to rebuild the facility.

NASA officials could finally relax. It appeared there was no way the Soviets could do anything to upstage the crowning glory of the U.S. space program—the moon launch scheduled for July. But their tenacious rivals pulled one last ace from their sleeve. On July 13, four days before *Apollo 11* was to launch, the Soviets shot *Luna 15* streaking toward the moon. Anxious U.S. officials asked the Soviets for an explanation. They were told not to worry; the unmanned *Luna 15* would not interfere with the U.S. mission in any way. What they did not say was that their goal was to land the ship on the moon, have it collect dirt samples off the surface, and rush home with the prize before *Apollo 11* landed.

HISTORIC FLIGHT

On July 17, 1969, Neil Armstrong, Buzz Aldrin, and Michael Collins rode the elevator to their spaceship on top of the towering Saturn V rocket. Although thrilled with the opportunity, they recognized the dangers and the possibility of a failed mission. Collins estimated that this historic flight had a fifty-fifty chance of success.

In Armstrong's words, "Although confident, we were certainly not overconfident. In research and exploration, the unexpected is always expected. We would not have been surprised if a malfunction

---

THE SPACE RACE'S "PEARL HARBOR"

On the eve of the Apollo 11 *moon landing, NASA director Thomas O. Paine summed up his view of the U.S.-Soviet space race in views expressed in the July 7, 1969, issue of* U.S. News & World Report.

"I think Russia's first Sputnik—which was a sort of 'space Pearl Harbor'—startled us and raised some basic questions: whether we really were the adventurous people we thought we were; and whether we actually had the technical preeminence we thought we had.

The manned landing on the moon, in a sense, is the culmination of America's satisfying everyone that it is indeed the leading technological nation that everyone thought it was before Sputnik blazed across the skies."

(Above) Astronauts Neil Armstrong, Michael Collins, and Buzz Aldrin blast off for the moon aboard Apollo 11 on July 17, 1969 (right).

or an unforeseen occurrence prevented a successful moon landing. We knew that hundreds of thousands of Americans had given their best. Now it was time for us to give our best."[60]

At 9:32 A.M. their thundering Saturn rocket hurled them into space. Two hours and forty-two minutes later, they were given clearance to go to the moon. Boosting their velocity to over twenty-five thousand miles per hour, they broke clear of the earth's gravity and headed on a seventy-three-hour voyage to immortality.

While they were in route, *Luna 15* braked into lunar orbit. Twice it responded to remote instructions putting it into lower orbit. Rushing to beat *Apollo 11*, *Luna 15* approached its final descent to the moon's surface.

PROGRAM ALARM

As it approached the moon, *Apollo 11* slowed to let the lunar gravity pull it into orbit. On July 20 Armstrong and Aldrin moved into the LM, named the *Eagle*, and pulled loose from the command module *Columbia*. The *Eagle* descended facedown, going backward. Armstrong stood at the controls while Aldrin monitored the complex, battery-operated computer that performed the radar, environmental control system, and main guidance functions.

As NASA control listened breathlessly, the *Eagle* descended to six thousand feet. Suddenly Aldrin alerted Mission Control in Houston to a computer program alarm, number 1202. Neither Aldrin nor Armstrong knew what the 1202 alarm given by the computer signified. The only one who did was a twenty-seven-year-old technician named Steve Bales. All eyes at Mission Control in Houston flew to Bales. The descent schedule was intricately timed. Whatever was wrong had to be determined and corrected immediately. Bales performed some quick calculations and calmly told the flight director to ignore the warning. It simply meant that the computer was so overloaded that it was recycling so that it could keep handling incoming data.

The astronauts now faced the riskiest part of the adventure. No one had ever

On the moon, Buzz Aldrin stands next to the American flag (left). A footprint in the lunar soil marks "one giant leap for mankind" (right).

SECRET TERROR

The Apollo 11 *moon flight was far from a cold, calculated, sterilized, computer-controlled operation. In* Man on the Moon: The Voyages of the Apollo Astronauts, *Andrew Chaikin captures the element of risk that surrounded the launching of the* Eagle *from the surface of the moon to rejoin Michael Collins orbiting in* Columbia.

"Armstrong and Aldrin stood side by side at the *Eagle*'s controls, helmets and gloves locked into place. The first launch from another world was two minutes away. . . .

To Aldrin, the thought of being stranded on the moon forever simply didn't exist. To conjure that dark thought would have been to go against the whole philosophy behind the mission: Everything had been stacked to ensure their success.

But inside *Columbia*, Mike Collins could not be so confident. Lunar orbit seemed remarkably safe compared to the spot Armstrong and Aldrin were in. Perched motionless on the surface with a single rocket engine to get them off, they belonged to the moon. The engine must work, and it must work long enough for *Eagle* to reach some kind of orbit. . . .

As he waited for lift-off, Collins could no longer push aside his darkest fears. 'My secret terror for the last six months,' he would later write, 'has been leaving them on the moon and returning alone; now I am within minutes of finding out the truth of the matter. If they fail to rise from the surface, or crash back into it, I am not going to commit suicide; I am coming home forthwith, but I will be a marked man for life.'"

tried to land anything on the moon, much less an odd contraption like the LM. As Armstrong descended toward his designated landing spot, he saw that they were heading for a boulder field. At the same time, a red warning light told him he had less then two minutes of fuel remaining.

Armstrong was no stranger to hazardous flying. He had cheated death on at least two occasions, once when he was shot down on a mission over Korea and the second when he ejected just before his LM simulator crashed on a training flight. Armstrong's parachute had opened with less than half a second to spare. Now he steeled his nerves to concentrate on avoiding boulders and craters and finding a safe place to land. He dropped to within three hundred feet of the surface when he had to

The Eagle *lunar module approaches the* Columbia *command module after lifting off from the moon. There was some risk that Armstrong and Aldrin would be stranded on the lunar surface.*

tilt the LM to avoid a large crater. Hovering above the surface, he finally found a favorable spot and coolly touched down with less than thirty seconds of fuel to spare.

Some seven hours later, Armstrong opened the hatch on the LM and stepped down the ladder. "That's one small step for man, one giant leap for mankind,"[61] he declared as he placed his foot on the moon.

Only one part of Kennedy's challenge remained before the United States could enjoy its space victory: they had to bring the astronauts back alive. After a busy few hours on the moon, during which Aldrin and Armstrong cavorted in the weak gravity of the moon, performed experiments, and collected forty-five pounds of soil and rock, they reentered the LM. The ascent

stage was disengaged from the descent stage and the module was prepared for takeoff.

Again NASA officials felt their hearts coming out of their chests. There had been no safe way of performing a test launch of the module from the moon, and there was no backup system. If, for any reason, the rocket failed to ignite and perform perfectly, Armstrong and Aldrin were stranded on the moon.

But the rocket did ignite and the *Eagle* lifted off. Soon they linked up with Collins in the *Columbia* and were on their way home. The very next day, *Luna 15*, whose controls had failed so close to its target, crashed into the moon. On July 24 *Columbia* splashed safely down in the South Pacific Ocean. The race to the moon was over.

From Competition to Cooperation

Shortly after Armstrong set foot on the moon, a jubilant Wernher von Braun predicted that humans would walk on Mars by 1980. But it was not to be. For as Wayne Lee wrote, "Although the technology existed for a Mars trip, the national will did not."[62]

Long before the moon landing, U.S. government officials and citizens had questioned the sense of spending so much money for something that gave so little tangible return. For although space program advocates argued that technology advances spawned by aerospace research benefited the public by producing improvements in transportation, safety, materials, and computers, the public and government cost-cutters remained skeptical. The trip to the moon had required the efforts of 34,000 NASA employees, 100,000 scientists and technicians, 377,000 subcontractor employees from 20,000 U.S. business firms, and carried a final price tag of $24 billion.

Even in the last years of the Apollo program, government support for space research had dwindled. NASA's budget had been pared from $5.25 billion in 1965 to $3.991 billion the year of the moon landing. President Nixon was urged by some advisers to end the space program on the high note of *Apollo 11*'s success.

Nixon did continue the Apollo program, which sent six more successful missions to the moon over the next two and a half years. But by 1972 the momentum that carried astronauts far out into space was over. The United States began to concentrate its efforts on a space shuttle and unmanned flights to distant planets as well as a space station. The Soviet Union focused primarily on building a space station.

Once the goal of a moon landing was achieved, the space race fizzled. Well before the fall of the Berlin Wall and the thawing of the Cold War at the end of the 1980s, the two competing nations decided that cooperation was more cost-effective than competition in space research. In 1975 U.S. astronauts Tom Stafford, Vance Brand, and Deke Slayton rendezvoused and docked with a

Rivals become colleagues. After docking the Apollo and Soyuz capsules (left), astronauts Tom Stafford, Aleksei Leonov, and Deke Slayton join together in a new age of U.S.-Soviet space cooperation (right).

Soviet spaceship manned by Aleksei Leonov and Valeri Kubasov. Their two days of joint experiments raised the curtain on a new era of U.S.-Soviet space cooperation.

That cooperation was never more apparent than in November 2000, when a U.S. company, One Stop Satellite Solutions (OSSS), signed an agreement with the Russian company Kosmotras. Under the terms of the deal, OSSS would purchase Russian SS-19s, missiles formerly armed and pointed at the United States, as launchers for a series of commercial satellites.

Manned Flights During the Space Race

USSR			USA		
Date	Spacecraft	Cosmonauts	Date	Spacecraft	Astronauts
4-12-61	*Vostok 1*	Gagarin			
			5-5-61	*Freedom 7*	Shepard
			7-21-61	*Liberty Bell 7*	Grissom
8-6-61	*Vostok 2*	Titov			
			2-20-62	*Friendship 7*	Glenn
			5-24-62	*Aurora 7*	Carpenter
8-11-62	*Vostok 3*	Nikolayev			
8-12-62	*Vostok 4*	Popovich			
			1-3-63	*Sigma 7*	Schirra
			5-15-63	*Faith 7*	Cooper
6-14-63	*Vostok 5*	Bykovsky			
6-16-63	*Vostok 6*	Tereshkova			
10-12-64	*Voskhod 1*	Komarov Feoktistov Yegorov			
3-18-65	*Voskhod 2*	Belyayev Leonov			
			3-23-65	*Gemini 3*	Grissom Young
			6-3-65	*Gemini 4*	McDivitt White
			8-21-65	*Gemini 5*	Cooper Conrad
			12-4-65	*Gemini 7*	Borman Lovell
			12-15-65	*Gemini 6*	Schirra Stafford
			3-16-66	*Gemini 8*	Armstrong Scott
			6-3-66	*Gemini 9*	Stafford Cernan
			7-18-66	*Gemini 10*	Young Collins

USSR			USA		
Date	Spacecraft	Cosmonauts	Date	Spacecraft	Astronauts
			9-12-66	*Gemini 11*	Conrad Gordon
			11-11-66	*Gemini 12*	Lovell Aldrin
4-28-67	*Soyuz 1*	Komarov			
			10-11-68	*Apollo 7*	Schirra Cunningham Eisele
10-26-68	*Soyuz 3*	Beregovoy			
			12-21-68	*Apollo 8*	Borman Lovell Anders
1-14-69	*Soyuz 4*	Shatalov			
1-15-69	*Soyuz 5*	Volynov Khrunov Yeliseyev			
			3-3-69	*Apollo 9*	McDivitt Scott Schweickart
			5-18-69	*Apollo 10*	Stafford Young Cernan
			7-17-69	*Apollo 11*	Armstrong Aldrin Collins

Notes

Introduction: Sparks of the Space Race

1. Wernher von Braun and Frederick Ordway II, *History of Rocketry and Space Travel*. New York: Thomas Y. Crowell, 1975, p. 18.

2. Quoted in von Braun and Ordway, *History of Rocketry and Space Travel*, p. 41.

3. Quoted in Nathan Aaseng, *Twentieth Century Inventors*. New York: Facts On File, 1991, p. 28.

Chapter 1: Military Interest in Rockets

4. Quoted in T. A. Heppenheimer, *Countdown: A History of Space Flight*. New York: John Wiley & Sons, 1997, p. 14.

5. Quoted in William B. Breuer, *Race to the Moon: America's Duel with the Soviets*. Westport, CT: Praeger, 1993, p. 11.

6. Quoted in Nathan Aaseng, *Breaking the Sound Barrier*. New York: Julian Messner, 1992, p. 30.

7. Quoted in Breuer, *Race to the Moon*, p. 60.

8. Quoted in Heppenheimer, *Countdown*, p. 38.

Chapter 2: The U.S.-Soviet Missile Race

9. Quoted in Heppenheimer, *Countdown*, p. 67.

10. Quoted in Breuer, *Race to the Moon*, p. 76.

11. Quoted in Breuer, *Race to the Moon*, p. 84.

12. "Journey into Space," *Time*, December 8, 1952, p. 62.

13. Quoted in "Journey into Space," p. 64.

14. Quoted in "Journey into Space," p. 70.

Chapter 3: The Satellite Race

15. Quoted in James Schefter, *The Race: The Uncensored Story of How America Beat Russia to the Moon*. New York: Doubleday, 1999, p. 5.

16. Quoted in Heppenheimer, *Countdown*, p. 101.

17. Quoted in Breuer, *Race to the Moon*, p. 135.

18. Quoted in "The Special Threat," *Time*, October 14, 1957, p. 22.

19. Quoted in "The Special Threat," p. 22.

20. Quoted in Schefter, *The Race*, p. 20.

21. Quoted in "Red Moon over the U.S.," *Time*, October 14, 1957, p. 27.

22. Quoted in "Red Moon over the U.S.," p. 27.

23. Quoted in "The Special Threat," p. 23.

24. Quoted in "The Special Threat," p. 21.

25. Quoted in "The Special Threat," p. 22.

26. Quoted in "The Special Threat," p. 22.

27. Quoted in Schefter, *The Race*, p. 36.

28. Quoted in Heppenheimer, *Countdown*, p. 155.

Chapter 4: The Race for Manned Spaceflight

29. Quoted in Charles Murray and Catherine Bly Cox, *Apollo: The Race to the Moon*. New York: Simon & Schuster, 1989, p. 31.

30. Quoted in Schefter, *The Race*, p. 88.

31. Quoted in Walter Cunningham, *The All-American Boys*. New York: Macmillan, 1977, p. 58.

32. Edwin Diamond, "How to Lose the Space Race," *Newsweek*, October 19, 1959, p. 73.

33. Quoted in Schefter, *The Race*, p. 112.

34. Quoted in Murray and Cox, *Apollo*, p. 67.

35. Quoted in Heppenheimer, *Countdown*, p. 162.

36. Quoted in Breuer, *Race to the Moon*, p. 3.

37. Quoted in Schefter, *The Race*, p. 133.

38. Quoted in Murray and Cox, *Apollo*, p. 14.

Chapter 5: Reaching Toward the Moon

39. Quoted in Wayne Lee, *To Rise from Earth*. New York: Facts On File, 2000, p. 114.

40. Quoted in Murray and Cox, *Apollo*, p. 112.

41. Quoted in "Journey into Space," p. 63.

42. Quoted in Murray and Cox, *Apollo*, p. 127.

43. Quoted in Schefter, *The Race*, p. 181.

44. Quoted in Schefter, *The Race*, p. 205.

45. Quoted in Lee, *To Rise from Earth*, p. 117.

46. Quoted in Lee, *To Rise from Earth*, p. 121.

47. Quoted in Schefter, *The Race*, p. 235.

48. Quoted in von Braun and Ordway, *History of Rocketry and Space Travel*, p. 215.

Chapter 6: The Grand Prize

49. Schefter, *The Race*, p. 245.

50. Quoted in "How the U.S. Beat Russia to the Moon," *U.S. News & World Report*, July 7, 1969, p. 34.

51. Quoted in Cunningham, *The All-American Boys*, p. 12.

52. Quoted in Murray and Cox, *Apollo*, p. 220.

53. Quoted in Lee, *To Rise from Earth*, p. 137.

54. Quoted in Schefter, *The Race*, p. 249.

55. Quoted in Murray and Cox, *Apollo*, p. 223.

56. Quoted in "How the U.S. Beat Russia," p. 33.

57. "Poised for a Great Adventure," *Newsweek*, October 14, 1968, p. 66.

58. Quoted in "Poised for a Great Adventure," p. 71.

59. Quoted in Heppenheimer, *Countdown*, p. 238.

60. Quoted in Breuer, *Race to the Moon*, p. 187.

61. Quoted in von Braun and Ordway, *History of Rocketry and Space Travel*, p. 237.

Epilogue: From Competition to Cooperation

62. Lee, *To Rise from Earth*, p. 4.

For Further Reading

Nathan Aaseng, *Breaking the Sound Barrier*. New York: Julian Messner, 1992. Tells the story of the beginnings of rocket research from the standpoint of the daring pilots who tried to use its technology to break the sound barrier.

Franklin M. Branley, *From Sputnik to Space Shuttles*. New York: Thomas Y. Crowell, 1986. Simple text with a heavily illustrated look at the space efforts of various nations.

Andrew Chaikin, *Man on the Moon: The Voyages of the Apollo Astronauts*. New York: Viking, 1994. Longer and more complex than young adult-books, this behind-the-scenes look at the Apollo program and astronauts who went to the moon is fascinating enough to hold younger readers' attention.

Wayne Lee, *To Rise from Earth*. New York: Facts On File, 2000. A current, complete, informative, and well-illustrated treatment of the entire space program in a coffee table format rather than a story.

Alan Shepard and Deke Slayton, *Moon Shot*. Atlanta: Turner Publishing, 1994. In-depth, personal view of the space program from two of the original seven astronauts.

Carole Stott, *Space Exploration*. New York: Alfred Knopf, 1997. Profusely illustrated, this book touches on a large number of space topics.

Works Consulted

Nathan Aaseng, *Twentieth Century Inventors*. New York: Facts On File, 1991. Includes a chapter on U.S. rocket pioneer Robert Goddard.

"As Spacemen Look Beyond the Moon," *U.S. News & World Report*, July 7, 1967.

William B. Breuer, *Race to the Moon: America's Duel with the Soviets*. Westport, CT: Praeger, 1993. This book concentrates heavily on the early days of the space race, particularly the U.S. and Soviet efforts to obtain German rocket technology.

Walter Cunningham, *The All-American Boys*. New York: Macmillan, 1977. Personalized view of an Apollo astronaut of the U.S. space program.

Ed Diamond, "How to Lose the Space Race," *Newsweek*, October 19, 1959.

T. A. Heppenheimer, *Countdown: A History of Space Flight*. New York: John Wiley & Sons, 1997. Very detailed look at the space race, with particular focus on its beginnings.

"How the U.S. Beat Russia to the Moon," *U.S. News & World Report*, July 7, 1969.

"Journey into Space," *Time*, December 8, 1952.

John M. Logsdon, *The Decision to Go to the Moon*. Chicago: University of Chicago Press, 1966. A detailed analysis of the U.S. policy toward space exploration that led to the effort to put an astronaut on the moon.

Charles Murray and Catherine Bly Cox, *Apollo: The Race to the Moon*. New York: Simon & Schuster, 1989. This book relies more on a vignette approach rather than a chronological narrative to give background on the Apollo program.

"Orderly Formula," *Time*, October 28, 1957.

"Poised for a Great Adventure," *Newsweek*, October 14, 1968.

"Red Moon over the U.S.," *Time*, October 14, 1957.

James Schefter, *The Race: The Uncensored Story of How America Beat Russia to the Moon*. New York: Doubleday, 1999. Complete and up-to-date, this includes a great deal of recently revealed information about the Soviet space program.

"The Special Threat," *Time*, October 14, 1957.

Wernher von Braun and Frederick Ordway II, *History of Rocketry and Space Travel*. New York: Thomas Y. Crowell, 1975. History of the space race from the viewpoint of the most celebrated rocket scientist of all time.

Index

Picture Credits

Cover photo: NASA

APA/Archive Photos, 75

Archive Photos, 11, 15, 43

© Austrian Archives/Corbis, 14

© Bettmann/Corbis, 9, 20, 21, 25, 26, 32, 38, 42, 46, 48, 58, 62, 67 (right), 73, 83, 84, 86 (left), 91 (right), 96 (both)

© Corbis, 18, 79, 86 (right)

Digital Stock, 28

© Farrell Grehan/Corbis, 69

Library of Congress, 52

NASA, 34, 60, 63, 65, 67 (left), 68, 80, 89, 92 (both), 94

Popperfoto/Archive Photos, 91 (left)

© Rykoff Collection/Corbis, 76

Smithsonian, 53

© Underwood & Underwood/Corbis, 49

About the Author

Nathan Aaseng is the author of more than 150 books for young readers on a wide variety of subjects. More than three dozen of his works have won awards. A former microbiologist with a degree in biology and English from Luther College (Iowa), he currently lives in Eau Claire, Wisconsin, with his wife and four children.